# THE SHEPHERD OF WEEPINGWOLD

# THE SHEPHERD
# OF WEEPINGWOLD

By
**ENID DINNIS**

**ST. AIDAN PRESS**
Morning View, Kentucky

The Shepherd of Weepingwold.

First published in 1929 by B. Herder Book Company, St. Louis, MO.

Typesetting, layout and cover design copyright 2017 St. Aidan Press.*

Cover art by Andrea England.

ISBN-13: 978-0-9719230-5-8
ISBN-10: 0-9719230-5-1


For more information, contact:
www.staidanpress.com
staidanpress@gmail.com

* Text reset and proofread in 2023. No change has been made from the 1929 text except to correct mistakes in spelling and punctuation.

# CONTENTS

To
LUCILLE BORDEN

# THE SHEPHERD
# OF WEEPINGWOLD

## Chapter I

### *Weepingwold*

IR ROBERT LUFFKYN, merchant, Grand Master of the worshipful Company of Skinners, was riding with an escort suited to his dignity through the aptly named tract of desolation known as Weepingwold. A century-and-a-half back Weepingwold had been a flourishing village with its manor, its feudal lord and its strictly domiciled sons of the soil. Robert Luffkyn's grandfather had been one of the latter, a serf bound by the law to contribute to the cultivation of the land—the grand master of the Skinners Company was inordinately proud of the fact—but the Death, the scourge which had carried off a third of the population, so it was reckoned, had set the serfs a-wandering. The labourer, having through the scarcity of his species, become worthy of a princely hire, had proclaimed himself a freeman. Robert Luffkyn's grandfather had gone his own way and become a tanner. His son had developed the calling and amassed much money; and the grandson, Robert Luffkyn, by a dextrous business instinct, had become one of the richest merchants in the kingdom.

Robert Luffkyn not only dealt in hides; he extended his interest in the produce after the hides had become shoes—I beg pardon—shoon. In a sense he might have been called Robert the shoemaker and it would have gratified the peculiar kind of snobbery which the grandson of Robin the serf suffered from. At the present moment he was prospecting a still further application of the industry in which the family fortune had been made, as well as indulging a caprice arising out of his family pride.

Leather is required for the binding of books and Robert Luffkyn had heard rumours of a new invention by which the multiplication of books might be looked for in the near future. The astute man of commerce had heard stories of the "imprinting press" and it had caused him to dream dreams. In his dreams he visualised—cows, herds of cows, whose hides would supply leather for the binding of many books. With the contents of the books he was not concerned. He presumed they would be pious books—the lewd layman would still get his stories from the minstrel. Robert Luffkyn approved of pious books. Had not the worshipful Company of Skinners, the most pious of the city guilds, made him their grand master? Of the making of books there would be no end, and in consequence of the binding of the same.

Such was the larger dream of "Rob the tanner" (they had really nick-named him that—the supercilious lordlings), as he rode out to Weepingwold the cradle of his race.

But the reason for establishing his new tannery at Weepingwold had nothing commercial in it. It was just one of those whims and fancies that a wealthy man loves to indulge in when he has exhausted the normal luxuries of life. Luffkyn was determined to reestablish the Luffkyns on the soil which they had turned in the days of their servitude. At the present day the village of Weepingwold lay in desolation, its castle still inhabited by the last of the ancient race, Sir Hugh de Lessels. The property, now practically nil, had at length come into the market and Robert Luffkyn had hit upon the idea of becoming Lord of the Manor and restoring Weepingwold to its former place in the scheme of things under entirely new auspices.

There would be cows instead of corn, and a flourishing colony of tanners and other artificers in place of the husbandmen. Robert Luffkyn sent an agent to prospect on the possibilities of Weepingwold. The report was satisfactory. Old Sir Hugh de Lessels was in his dotage, and dying. The transfer of the remnant of his ancestral holding to the new owner could be accomplished through the bailiff (it may have been the franklin who officiated, but one can learn that from any reliable text book of the period so why waste time?) So Robert Luffkyn entered into possession, with all the Luciferlike and, withal, unrebuked pride of the self-made man. The last of the feudal land-owners might sit in his mouldering hall and exclaim, "soothly my ancestors were fine fellows!" but Sir Robert Luffkyn intended to place himself in a setting which would proclaim the fine fellow to be Robert Luffkyn himself. The very land which his grandfather had ploughed would call out, "Thou'rt a fine fellow, Rob Luffkyn!"

No wonder Robert Luffkyn rode into Weepingwold with his really fine head held well in the air.

The ancient castle of the de Lessels came into view as they reached the crest of the incline. It had been a fine place in its day, and he, Robert Luffkyn, would make it a fine place again. Luffkynwold—that was to be the name of his new Eden—would have its baronial hall. Why not, if a baron didn't live in it? He would rebuild it in the new style. The time had passed for fortified dwellings and donjon keeps, and the like. Luffkynwold had a future before it in the new England which was replacing the old one.

For years the holder of the naked baronial rights, had lived in a desolation of withered glories, aged and decrepit, his scanty revenues mopped up by the grinding taxes imposed by the close-fisted Tudor monarch who was ever in his parlour counting out his money.

As far as anyone seemed to know Sir Hugh was the last of his race, the family which had founded the manor of Weepingwold in far away times before the world had begun to weep. A forerunner of the Black Death had carried off the bride of John de Lessels within a few days of their nuptials, and the tomb, out on the centre of the wold, where the desolate husband had elected to lay her remains had first given the wold its lugubrious name. When the great Death devastated the village they had made a burial ground round about the tomb, away from the dwellings. The tomb itself now stood empty, for a successor of John de Lessels had removed its contents to the more seemly precincts of the village church, but Weepingwold continued to shed immortal tears through the years that followed the great desolation.

The de Lessels family carried on a tradition of misfortune. Battle, murder and untimely death thinned out the branches of the family tree. Sir Hugh had several sons but all died without issue, save one, and his offspring, an only son, had perished in foreign parts, so it was said. It was presumably the last of the de Lessels whom Robert Luffkyn had taken over as a temporary and negligible detail, together with the obsolete glories of the baronial past. It was well that it should be so; it left the field clear for the new family. Sir Hugh was welcome to live out his numbered days in some corner where he could be stored, with the faded tapestries. The Grand Master of the worshipful Company of Skinners was nothing if not magnanimous.

It might surely be taken that luck had turned for Weepingwold with the advent of this man of benefactions who, rumour said, was richer than the king who counted out his, and other peoples' money.

There was an old rhyme that ran:

> "When Weepingwold hath a laughing lord
> Treasure of gold shall he watch and ward."

But however much of gold there might be about Robert Luffkyn there was nothing of laughter. An immense gravity marked the man of large designs. Laughter is for women no less than tears, was a favourite saying of his, and even when he indulged in a certain dry humour, his countenance remained sphinxlike and imperturbable.

Luffkyn's guide, a heavy visaged native, pointed to the right of them. "Yonder lies the church," he said. "Farmer Roger useth it to shelter his cattle."

The church was a sturdy grey building with a squat tower, that had stood for centuries and served its holy purpose so long as a pastor had been forthcoming.

Sir Robert ran his eye over the dilapidated walls. "I shall have need of a church," he said, reflectively, "and a curate."

"There hath been no parson this hundred years," the guide replied. "The church house scarcely hath a wall standing."

"It will have four walls and a parson inside it, before thy next babe is in its cradle," was the crisp reply.

The guide—he was a hogger with nineteen children—looked unconvinced. "Small use a church house without a church," he opined.

"But there will be a church. I intend to use the church."

Hodge the hogger answered crisply in his turn:

"Thou can'st not. Farmer Roger useth it for his cattle."

"Farmer Roger will shelter his cattle elsewhere."

Hodge the hogger shook his head a second time.

"But his father sheltered his cattle there before him," he said.

The man of international negotiations (in the matter of pelts) surveyed the speaker. He surveyed the mule upon which he was riding. Then he shrugged his shoulders. The peasant was on a par with his mount. One doesn't explain away "insuperable difficulties" to a mule.

"There be no priests round about," the hogger went on. "And no Mass, save at the churches where the monks from Bycross say a Mass ever and anon."

5

"Where is Bycross?" Sir Robert asked.

"'Tis across the wold. The monks be praying men, but some of them be priests and can say Mass. They have the making of books as well as the tilling of the ground, but mostly they be praying men."

Robert Luffkyn made a mental note. "You can guide me to Bycross anon," he said.

.        .        .        .        .

The clipper-clopper of a cavalcade of riders was seldom heard now-a-days in the courtyard of Weepingwold castle. Sir Hugh de Lessels raised himself on to one elbow in bed to listen. His hearing was still fairly keen and the sound penetrated his memory as well as his ear. Perhaps it ignored the ear as a means of transit to Sir Hugh's inner consciousness?

"What was that?" he said. "Who comes to Weepingwold?"

The question was addressed to Thomas, his all-round man who carried on the anachronism of the "retainer," for retainers in the strictly feudal sense were out of date. Had Tom Vertlet been of his age he would have walked off long since to seek his fortune in the world of opening wonders; as it was he permitted himself to be retained. The aged man who lay on the bed in the stone chamber in the round tower retained every particle of Thomas Vertlet. Tom it was who waited on him, hand and foot. When Death lifted the ragged velvet curtain and peeped across the threshold at Sir Hugh, as it sometimes did, Tom would ride off in haste to Bycross Priory and fetch the good Prior to give his master the comforts of religion, for Weepingwold had no chaplain of its own in these days. Priests were too direfully scarce. The Death had swept them off by the thousands and the new generation found its vocation in commerce rather than in the service of souls. So the good Prior did his best for the knight of Weepingwold. True, the latter had bequeathed the main bulk of his property to Bycross Priory but since the goods and chattels bequeathed had long since ceased to exist the Prior could hardly be charged with an interested motive. Like Thomas, his services were for love.

"Who comes to Weepingwold?"

Thomas would fain have parried the question. He would have preferred that Sir Hugh had not been made aware of the new arrival. Weepingwold had changed owners, with all that it contained. Certain deeds had been duly signed by Sir Hugh de Lessels but the incident had passed gently from his infirm mind. The new owner, Sir Robert Luffkyn, had behaved as became a man of such notorious benevolence. "Let be, let be!" he had said, with a wave of his hand. "There will be room enow at Weepingwold for one that ever lies a-bed. Hustle not the old man to his grave miscomfortably."

So Sir Hugh remained in the damp regality of the vaulted chamber in the fortified corner of the ancient pile.

All the same, the presence of the new owner would need to be explained sooner or later; and here he was arrived on the scene!

"'Tis one Robert Luffkyn that comes seeking entertainment," Tom made cautious reply. "But he hath given due warning and all is in readiness."

The destitute man on the bed laid his head back on the silken pillow. "Luffkyn?" he repeated, "there were Luffkyns who worked on the land when I was a lad. Rob Luffkyn was branded by my grandfather for a fugitive, but he made off again. A rogue and vagabond, he was, that would not be bound to the soil."

Tom Vertlet was plainly disquieted by the freshness of the old man's memory. What if Sir Hugh, this fierce and terrifying old man on the bed, got to know that Weepingwold had passed into the hands of one of the servile race?

It was too late to try to lead the speaker's thoughts into a safer direction. Already there were steps on the stone stairs. The newcomer had lost no time in presenting himself to the late proprietor. He was ushered in by John Appleyard, his man of business.

Robert Luffkyn stood there, a well-set up man of about fifty with blunt features, a piercing eye, and a mouth that shut very tightly. He was magnificently garbed in a fur-lined travelling coat, and there was a ring on his finger which represented wealth in itself. It was what would be termed a commanding presence, and it commanded by right of ownership.

The price that Robert Luffkyn had paid for the manor had gone to pay off the accumulated debt to the crown. The old man with the ivory-coloured face on the bed was destitute.

The blurred eyes in the wrinkled countenance scrutinised the new-comer. They were not unfriendly but somehow they found fault.

"There were Luffkyns on the land here—my land," the old man commented, reflectively, "that were fine fellows until one of them became a vagabond. My grandfather branded him with an iron, but he went off anon. Thou'rt a fine fellow, but thy fine feathers ill-become thee."

The sunken eyes moved critically over the figure with the fine feathers. Tom Vertlet went cold in the marrow of his spine. Robert Luffkyn remained mask-like in his expression.

"The vagabond that wandered forth was my grandfather," he said, "and the wandering forth brought him small harm in the end." The rays of the setting sun flashed on the ring on his finger. The last of the de Lessels lay there at his mercy, waiting to learn how little harm the wandering forth had done to the family of the fugitive serf.

The old man on the bed—Robert Luffkyn's bed—surveyed the speaker with the interest that one bestows on a new horse or a peculiar breed of dog.

"Then he begot a fine son ere he mounted the gallows," he said, "if thy father were as fine a man as thee. But," he trailed off peevishly—"the fine feathers make but a fool of thee. There were sumptuary laws when I was young. Fur and velvet, forsooth!"

Robert Luffkyn fixed the eye that could sum up the value of a cow's hide to a nicety on the face on the pillow—his pillow, be it remembered. The retainer waited for what was to come, shaking in what were, now one comes to think of it, Robert Luffkyn's shoes since he held his livery from his lord.

Luffkyn answered.

"Shall I tell you what Rob Luffkyn's grandson possesses in addition to feathers?" he enquired. "The law of the land hath not prevented Rob Luffkyn's grandson from becoming master of——"

The man on the bed was not listening. His eyes travelled beyond the speaker and were fixed on something at the end of the room. Luffkyn followed the gaze without finishing his sentence. The curtain over the entrance had been withdrawn and a little girl of about eight years old stood there, peeping in. She was quaintly dressed in faded silk garments. She stood there just inside the door, very erect. Out of a delicate little face, a pair of immense grey eyes, deep set and rather wide apart, took stock of Robin Luffkyn's grandson.

"Who is this?" the latter asked, eyeing the imperious little figure. The inventory had not included: "Item: one little girl in silk gown (faded)."

A woman came hastening in at the tail of her charge. She was about to answer the question but she was forestalled.

"I am Dame Petronilla de Lessels. Who be thou?"

She did not wait for an answer but continued, "I have come to see my grandfather because he is going to God and he has no priest."

The nurse intervened. "'Tis Sir Hugh's little great-granddaughter," she explained, hurriedly. "I am taking her to the nuns this Friday."

Luffkyn glanced interrogatively at John Appleyard.

"Sir Hugh's youngest grandson brought her here as a babe," he said. "His wife had gone off by herself, and the child was left. The nuns at Gracerood will look after her. She is the last of her race."

The child who had thus been introduced as the last of her race, continued to take stock of the stranger, much in the way her forebear on the bed had done. There was a likeness in bearing, if not in feature, between the two.

Luffkyn turned to the bailiff. "Dame Petronilla de Lessels was not included in the inventory," he observed, drily. "The escheator's clerk hath been careless."

"I will take her to the nuns," the nurse put in, hastily. "They owe much to Weepingwold. They will not refuse her bread and lodging."

The sick man had settled back on his pillow. His eyes were closed. Petronilla had crept up to the bed and was gazing at him with her great eyes. She turned round with a smile.

"I said the holy Name, and he is dreaming of Heaven," she said. Then she went up to Robert Luffkyn and surveyed him with what might be termed a kindly interest.

"I will go to the nuns," she said, "but when I am grown up I will return to Weepingwold because then it will belong to me."

The sick man had opened his eyes. "Bring me the ink-horn and pen," he cried. "I am wishful to add something to my will."

Thomas hastened over to him. Sir Hugh was ever changing or adding something to his will, and now he had chosen the present moment for renewing the grim mummery!

"Write it down," he said, straining his voice to effective utterance, "I bequeath my second-best pair of leather shoon to Rob Luffkyn that tills my land."

Luffkyn smiled grimly. "Take the ink-horn and set it down," he said to Thomas; then he turned his attention to little Dame Petronilla.

Dame Petronilla was amusing. She was unconsciously satirising the egregious pride of the ancient family.

"You might stay at Gracerood and be Lady Abbess," he suggested.

Petronilla deliberated. "Then I would make you my reeve," she said. "That is, if you would promise to be good to the poor people and the beggars and the lepers."

"I am well named as a friend of the needy," the new master of Weepingwold replied, "beg they never so haughtily."

The irony of the remark was lost on the person addressed although it entered into the soul of Thomas the retainer. The awkward situation had resolved itself into a grim little comedy. Dame Petronilla was still deliberating.

"And the dogs?" she queried, and eyed her reeve searchingly.

"My dog thinks the world of me, save that my neighbour hath a bone in his wallet."

The answer gave satisfaction. Petronilla approved her henchman. "I am not yet sure whether I want to be an Abbess," she said, "but you can look after Weepingwold while I am making up my mind."

The sick man was calling out, "Set it down. I bequeath my second-best pair of shoon to Rob Luffkyn that tills my land."

Robert Luffkyn strode over to the bedside. Vertlet trembled. But Luffkyn was experienced in many things besides tanning. He stood there saying nothing and the expression on his face had softened. Petronilla slipped over and stood beside him. She, too, gazed at the pallid face. There was no fear in the gaze, but amazing concentration. She touched the withered old hand on the coverlet lightly and stood there watching.

Sir Hugh closed his eyes. The strained look on his countenance relaxed. He opened them again. "I bequeath my soul to Almighty God," he murmured, "my soul to Almighty God."

Then a few moments later, his lips moved again but no sound came. The effort of making a will had given the *coup de grace* to the worn-out heart. Sir Hugh de Lessels had breathed his last. The only thing left to him to bequeath had fled to the One who had owned it all along.

"The angels are still there," Petronilla whispered. "I liked not the demons, but they ran away when he said the holy Name Jesus."

.        .        .        .        .

Death had opportunely relieved the new Lord of Weepingwold of his somewhat embarrassing encumbrance. Sir Hugh could be carried forth with all due honours to rest with his fathers. Luffkyn owed him no grudge for his bequest of a pair of second-hand shoon. If anything it ministered to the kind of pride that kept his chin well in the air. But there still remained the child. Sir Hugh had not been the last of his race after all.

Somehow this latter fact weighed on Robert Luffkyn's mind. The child might grow up to raise a new brood of de Lessels who would take the old name and cast eyes on Weepingwold and pose in the minds of its inhabitants as "the family." An extraordinary jealousy held him in its grip. A kind of fidgety fear. The dominant little dame might pass on her characteristics to the male line. The blood of leaders of men flowed in her veins.

The solution was plain. The dominant little lady must become an Abbess. He, Robert Luffkyn, would see to this at his early convenience.

# Chapter II

### *The Prior's Ewe-lamb*

DAM'S SWEAT lay thick on the youthful brow of Chris— there was more than that to his name, but it was too long for ordinary use—for the making of books in the scriptorium is every bit as laborious as working in the fields, even in the ordinary way, and Brother Kit, as he was usually called, had an additional reason for the sweat which accompanied his labour. He had discovered a mistake in the text of the copy of the scriptures upon which he was engaged. The mistake was three lines up and, horror of horrors!—it was a dropped negative, changing the sense of the text as though the Devil himself had handled the quill. For the last ten minutes the unspeakable error had remained there in the sight of the angels—it had been a stirring from his guardian angel which had enabled him to detect the error now.

The words stood there before him: "Thou shall steal."

Brother Kit smote his breast and sent up a prayer for forgiveness. Pumice stone, scalpel and a sharp razor lay at hand as well as quills and ink-horn. The scribe applied himself to the task of erasing the last three lines, written in the faultless penmanship of the cloister. It took up much time, and wasting time was an offence in itself. Why had his thoughts soared heavenward when they should have been on his work? He would confess his fault in chapter as well as to Brother Paul, the master of the scriptorium. Poor Brother Paul. How horrified he would be. The thought that the error might have remained undiscovered would cause the holy monk many sleepless nights. Why, even the heretics did not actually affirm a commandment, "thou shalt steal."

Brother Kit applied his razor to the parchment with vigour. A loud clanging at the door-bell made no impression on him. It was repeated—a prolonged and terrifying clang. Brother Kit sprang up. He remembered that the ancient door-keeper had begged him to keep watch during his absence in the infirmary, the priory was grievously short-handed in these lean days, and the brothers often had to fill more than one office.

Another defection! And Master Walter Hilton insisted in his book that contemplation can only be reached through the gate of solid virtues! Brother Kit made an unmonastic bolt for the door.

The bell was insistent. Whoever could it be? Visitors were rare in these days at Bycross Priory. In the old flourishing days they had been plentiful, but now-a-days guests consisted only of the poor who came in greater numbers than ever, but not with a clang of the bell like this.

Father Prior in his cell, poring over the latest demand from the king's escheater, likewise heard the clang. He had caught, moreover, the sound of horses' hoofs and it struck cold fear into his heart. In these days there was talk of suppressing some of the moribund religious houses and applying their revenues to collegiate purposes. Bycross might well have been marked down for such a purpose, for its community consisted of but a few monks, and those mainly elderly and most of them decrepit. There was only little Brother Chrysostom who belonged to the rising generation. He was minding the door now, and probably in an ecstasy, hence the prolonged clanging of the bell.

He had taken Tom the carter's son from the plough and made a monk of him because from infancy he had shown strong marks of a vocation. The small Kit had sung his prayers and told himself stories of the saints with an artless familiarity that marked him for the cloister. If a Christian will insist on singing his prayers to a cheerful ditty and frisking about with his angel guardian he will give less scandal in the cloister than any other place. Kit's baptismal name had needed supplementing. His two elder brothers had been respectively, Tom and Nat. Kit might be presumed to mean Christopher, but there was a Christopher already at the Priory so Kit had been religiously developed into Chrysostom, for Sunday use, Chrystogonus having been suggested and rejected, even for Sundays.

Father Prior was a gentle old scholar whose heart dwelt in his library when it was not in the chapel. His store of books consisted solely of works of theology and the philosophies approved by the Church, but he had taken wistful cognisance of the new learning, with its researches into "profane" literature and had cast longing thoughts in the direction of the volumes treating of the "humanities" of which he heard tell. Strange yearnings were in the soul of the Prior of Bycross. The Benedictines at Westminster, it was said, had found a new way of multiplying books without end. But few new books came his way.

The clanging of the bell had ceased. The visitors, whoever they might be, had been admitted.

The Priory had been famous in the old days before the Death for its scholarship, but now-a-days its very existence was threatened. Menacing visitors might arrive any day armed with authority from the diocesan. Bycross was not a relaxed house—his children led exemplary lives, he had indeed a saint in the making in little Brother Chrysostom—thank goodness the boy had answered the bell at last!—but one holy novice could not save a community.

The holy novice in question burst in upon his superior at this moment—an agitated Brother Kit, his thick, curly hair that should have been clipped much rumpled round the all-but obliterated tonsure that should have been shaved afresh.

"'Tis one that sayeth that he be Sir Robert Luffkyn," he gasped, "and he said it as though he had been His Grace the King himself."

"Sir Robert Luffkyn?" Yes, the Prior had certainly heard the name. It was that of a man of fabulous wealth and unmatched benevolence. Grand Master of the worshipful Company of Skinners that was called the Guild of the Most Holy Sacrament. What could he be wanting at Bycross? Why, surely the rumour must be true which said that he had purchased the lands of poor old Sir Hugh de Lessels.

Sir Robert Luffkyn was waiting in the great stone parlour which proclaimed the glory of other days. He was standing by the window surveying the stretch of grazing land. Bycross had many and varied possibilities. They were opening out to his alert perception as he stood there waiting for the Prior.

On the backs of the cows quietly grazing on the Prior's lands Luffkyn saw book covers in the embryo; whilst in the scriptorium through which he had just passed he had visualised a printing press which would supply at lightning speed the necessary adjunct to a book-cover. Sir Robert Luffkyn, in short, was inviting letters to become the handmaid of the tanning industry, and operate side by side, as it were, with the shoe-making trade. He had, indeed, a complete scheme in view which began with a cow and ended with a copy of Aristotle.

Amazing indeed were the things which the good Prior of Bycross sat listening to during the minutes following Sir Robert Luffkyn's introduction of himself.

The Prior learnt that it was the great man's intention to establish an extensive tanning industry on the soil where his forebears had formerly lived as serfs.

The Prior was approving. "It were good for humility to bear in mind one's small beginnings." Most luckily he didn't say this out loud. When he got an opportunity of speech it was to enquire after Sir Hugh de Lessels, who had seemed in a bad way when he last saw him.

"He died yesterday," Sir Robert said.

The Prior crossed himself and breathed a prayer. "And the child, what will become of the little Dame Petronilla?" he queried.

"She will be educated by the nuns at Gracerood at my charges," Sir Robert said. "She hath the makings of a mitred Abbess in her."

The Prior smiled. He was greatly edified by Sir Robert's generosity.

The latter returned to the main point. Bycross, he regretted to learn, had lost much of its ancient glory. It was his idea to revive the fortunes of the same by a proposal which he now laid before the Prior. The Prior had doubtless heard speak of the imprinting press, an invention for making books by the thousand. The Abbot of Westminster already possessed one, and it was his, Sir Robert's idea to set one up near Weepingwold so that book making in its entirety might be carried on. Sir Robert would see to the leather if Bycross would see to the imprinting of the books. He would bring Bycross to life, and restore its ancient glories.

The Prior sat listening, as one in a dream, to the crisp speech of the Londoner. "Bring Bycross to life!"

Sir Robert enlarged on his scheme. The making of books were best undertaken under monkish auspices. Wonderful manuscripts had been discovered at Constantinople, so he had been told; copies of these could be brought to Bycross to be multiplied.

The old scholar's eyes glistened. What was this he was hearing? The Prior would act as censor. The Luffkyn press would be unimpeachably orthodox (they had made bonfires of suspected works before now, a most wicked waste of good material). The press of Robert Luffkyn would likewise multiply all those pious works that were popular among the simple folk. The tears came into the Prior's eyes as he listened. And he had feared that this was an enemy!

Luffkyn went on to tell him about the projected tannery at Weepingwold. He would be importing men by the hundreds to work there. Weepingwold Church was to be restored for their accommodation. "For this purpose I shall need a priest," Robert Luffkyn said.

The Prior shook his head, sadly. "There be no priests to be had," he said. "Commerce hath claimed all the young men that erstwhile gave themselves to the service of God."

Then Robert Luffkyn came to the point.

"I look to you to supply me with a curate for Weepingwold," he said.

The Prior shook his head again. "I have none in orders save the twain that serve the parishes round," he said. "Mine, moreover, is a contemplative order. We do but preach with our hands in the making of books."

"We have already touched on the making of books," Sir Robert said, drily. "We will return to that subject when you have found me a parson for Weepingwold. Who have you in the house that is not already a priest that might be made one?"

"The brothers are all aged and infirm," the Prior replied.

"Who was the youth that opened the door to me just now? Why not make a priest of him?"

The Prior smiled in spite of himself. Robert Luffkyn had a flair for seeing the manufactured article in the raw material, but this was too absurd.

"Little Brother Chrysostom! He is barely twenty, and he hath no learning. He is ever in contemplation and lives half in Heaven. He is young in mind, even for his tender years, and I sometimes wonder if he will ever grow older. He is half an angel."

The Prior smiled again to himself. "Little Brother Kit!"

Robert Luffkyn turned the information over in his mind.

"The Bishop hath raised some as young as he to holy orders," he said. "Holiness is no unseemly quality in a priest. If the youth is half an angel, what more can be wanted?"

"He is barely tonsured, and he hath no theology," the Prior pleaded. He was grievously disquieted. Little Brother Kit! It was ridiculous! Not to be thought of. But Sir Robert Luffkyn, on the other hand, was not a man to be trifled with.

"We will make a *corona* of his tonsure," the latter said, "and teach him some theology." He bracketed the two processes almost as though a barber might have performed both.

"But the Bishop," the other stammered.

"I will see to the Bishop," the master skinner said, and added, "Weepingwold must have a parson even though he be half an angel."

The good Prior of Bycross was blinking his dreamy eyes at the man of ways and means. His gentle old face wore the expression of a hare that has its ears set back. What was he to say? This Grand Master of the Worshipful Company knew so much about the mess of pottage, how was he to explain to him the existence, let alone the nature, of the birthright? Bycross had ever been the home of cloistered and contemplative men. Little Brother Chrysostom, his singing bird, had received a great gift from Heaven that might be his only in the solitudes. He was the shorn lamb upon whom the south wind of God's grace had blown. He knew nothing of the world. Like a poet of a later day the Prior would fain have prayed the world to be nobler for the sake of little Brother Chrysostom.

Robert Luffkyn was expressing a wish to inspect the mouldering glories of Bycross. The Prior conducted his amazing visitor round the external parts. There was the fine Norman cloister where as many as fifty monks had driven the quill and handled the brush in the days gone by.

"'Tis a far-reaching sermon that the man at the printing press preaches with his hands," Luffkyn observed, as he measured the space with his eye. The Prior warmed to his task of guide. A great day was surely coming for Bycross.

The tour of inspection filled the brothers with apprehension. There was a rumour abroad that the Pope had granted a Bull permitting the dissolution of certain decayed houses and the appropriation of their monies for the education of clerks. That the visitor had but come to rob the Prior of his ewe-lamb was not yet known.

Robert Luffkyn approved of all that he saw. His purpose would be admirably served by Bycross. He outlined his scheme. It included the restoration of the magnificent church, now falling into decrepitude, and the endowment of the community. The making of books was an industry permitted by the rule; the Grand Master of the Guild of the Most Holy Sacrament certainly knew what he was talking about. It was only the matter of Brother Chrysostom.

Sir Robert reverted to Brother Chrysostom when he had come to an end of his inspection. He took the transference of the praying brother to a more active sphere of usefulness as a settled matter. The gentle Prior permitted his opposition to melt away. It rested now with the Bishop, who, of course, had the decision in his hands, and with Sir Robert Luffkyn, whose latest benefaction surpassed all previous ones, to move the Bishop. All that remained to Father Prior was to acquaint the ewe-lamb with the extraordinary fact that he was to become a shepherd.

Robert Luffkyn rode away from Bycross thoroughly satisfied with the result of his visit. He had found the place where the insides for his output of books could be manufactured under the aegis of religion. He had overcome the faint objections of the man with the gentle, scholar's face, whose dream he had worked into his scheme, with his genius for utilising all the material at hand, and he had obtained a parson for Weepingwold who would put the fear of the Lord into the hearts of his dependents, lest that dependence might vanish in the lawlessness of the age.

It was a well-conceived scheme that was to make the name of Luffkyn take root in the ancestral soil, in a fine avenging of the serfdom of the forebears of Rob of the branded brow. The name of de Lessels would belong only to the dead. It was welcome to remain on the tombs in the church. It might go to its death with the honours that a chivalrous victor pays to a defeated foe. It had been some-what of a shock to find that the line was not extinct, but no mat-ter—the last of the de Lessels should die a Lady Abbess. To effect this was the next preoccupation of the new Lord of Weepingwold.

. . . . .

Gracerood, the nunnery to the ultimate ruling of which Sir Robert Luffkyn had allocated the Dame Petronilla de Lessels was, like Bycross, a house of fallen splendours. For generations past the gentry had sent their daughters there to be educated by the nuns, for Gracerood had a fame that spread far. In spite of changed times, its present Abbess, Dame Hilda de Hinton, a lady of high lineage had carried on the dignified tradition. Her capacity for manage-ment enabled Gracerood to keep up appearances, with a gallantry that few suspected.

The dignity of its past and a certain air of ordered activity marked the historic nunnery of Gracerood. The portress who ad-mitted Sir Robert Luffkyn, was by no means flustered by the ar-rival. He was conducted to the state parlour, an apartment hung with tapestries and furnished with high-backed chairs. The tap-estries were faded, and the cushion on the settle had been deftly renovated with the needle. The observant eye of the visitor had remarked these and other signs of straitened means before the curtain was drawn and the Lady Abbess made her entry.

A pale woman of insignificant height glided in with a swift rather than a studied movement. Luffkyn was prepared for some-one more imposing. He proceeded to explain his business with his customary conciseness. Weepingwold had become his property, and its late owner's great-grand-daughter, Petronilla de Lessels, had been left on his hands. He had taken her over, in fact, with the other effects of the late Sir Hugh. The de Lessels were an ancient family and he was wishful to dispose of the child in becoming wise, although she was but a pauper.

The Abbess Hilda was sitting very straight up on the uncushioned chair. She appeared to sit straighter when the allusion to Petronilla de Lessels being a pauper was made.

Sir Robert hastened on. The lady had not, so far, been impressed. He was willing to pay a bountiful pension to the Abbess of Graceröod for the maintenance of the little item whom the escheater had overlooked. He named a sum. It was calculated to make the superior of any convent open her eyes, let alone one which had fallen on hard times.

The Abbess bowed acquiescence.

His idea, Sir Robert went on, was to have the child trained for the cloister.

The Abbess considered the point. "Hath she a religious temper of soul?" she asked, and added:

"I can take her, and gladly, as a pupil, but it remains to be seen if she be fitted for the cloister."

Luffkyn stared at her. He returned what he considered to be a relevant answer:

"In the case of Dame Petronilla being named as your successor, I would pay her such a dowry as would relieve your monastery of its embarrassments. I take it that your revenues are not what they were in the past?"

The Abbess Hilda's eyebrows were slightly arched by nature. They now rose till they touched the edge of her white wimple. "I must see the child," she said. "Her calling may be rather to the married state than the cloister."

"But I intend her call to be to the cloister."

The Abbess collected the twitching corners of her mouth into a straight line. Her folded hands rested on a patch in her flowing habit which Luffkyn had not noticed before.

"Then it would hardly be a divine call," said the Abbess Hilda.

Then she continued: "I am willing to receive Petronilla de Lessels for the same pension that it is my custom to ask. Indeed, I would willingly forego any pension, for the de Lessels have been good friends to Gracerood. But it remains to be found out whether she hath a call to the cloister."

Luffkyn sat and considered. He had been told that the Abbess of Gracerood was a character, but he had not been prepared for a character of this kind. He had never met such egregious independence.

"There are other nunneries," he observed, "that would be glad enough to take the child on my terms."

Suddenly the woman in front of him flamed up. Her pale face flushed. "That is too true," she said, "and 'tis the ruin of the religious houses that they take in those that have the love of the world in their hearts. It is not the office of the cloister to turn a key on the will to do that which is not of itself a sin."

Then she gave him a shrewd look. "Wherefore is it of such grave import to you that the Dame Petronilla enters the cloister? She will most probably marry and have children."

"I wished the last of the de Lessels to be Abbess of Gracerood," Luffkyn said. The spirit of masterfulness in him was up against this lady in the threadbare scapular who was immune to the monetary lure. He loved a steeplechase but he generally cleared his hurdle on a golden steed.

The lady of the patched habit regarded him, reflective, in her turn. What manner of man was this?

"At least you can send Petronilla here for a while," she suggested conciliatingly. "If she hath no calling to be—my successor, then place her where you will."

"I will send her hither tomorrow," Luffkyn said.

He rode homeward, asking himself which had won the day, he or the Abbess in the patched garment that appeared to have made her so impervious to the voice of reason and common-sense.

# Chapter III

## *The Ewe-lamb Becomes a Shepherd*

ROTHER Chrysostom loved gardening the best of all the odd jobs that came in his way. He was in the garden grubbing up weeds when a messenger in my Lord the Bishop's livery rode up to the priory.

Kit remained intent on his job. The clanging of the door bell did not interest him unless it was his business to answer it.

His mind was intent on a dream of the garden of God, a man might dig and dream without the attendant mishap being a grave one. "My sister, my spouse, is a garden enclosed," sang little Brother Kit. He opened his golden mouth and sang his canticle as he dug well into the roots of the weeds with his spud. He loved to sing his prayers, like the hermit of Hampole;—that is, when he was not telling himself stories, for the things around him had a way of speaking to him in parables. Brother Paul, his novice master, had once tried to teach him a method of prayer, for Brother Paul had a tidy mind. Brother Kit had come to him with the confession that he had spent his hour telling God stories. Brother Paul had changed the method, and the novice had come to him with a new scruple, God had been telling stories to him and he had only listened. He was singing out loud now, and inviting the south wind to blow through his garden so that the aroma of his lilies might be distributed, when the attenuated figure of Father Prior appeared in the distance. The Prior had a missive in his hand.

## The Ewe-lamb Becomes a Shepherd

There was a cruel task in front of the Prior. The Bishop had given his consent to the taking away of his ewe-lamb. The necessary dispensation was there. Within a few weeks Brother Kit would be regarded as ready to receive holy orders in their plenitude. He, the little door-keeper, whose tonsure had been a temporary decoration swiftly obliterated by the rough locks of Tom the carter's son! The task of getting sufficient Latin into the little brother's head would be prodigious. As to theology? Brother Chrysostom had no subtlety of intellect. He took the teaching of Holy Church as he took his breakfast, and as with his breakfast, thrived on the nourishment, and proclaimed its virtue by a healthful vigour of soul. But these matters did not vex the good Prior's soul in anything like the degree that this other thing did. It had been a direct call to the sheltered religious life that had caused him to take Tom Plimsett's son from the plough and make a clerk of him—save the mark! a little shock-headed urchin who was hurt by the sight and sound of sin ere he knew from whence the lash came. "My sister, my spouse, is a garden enclosed," Kit was singing. He had succeeded in getting up an obstinate clod. As obstinate as one's besetting sin, or the heresy that made men join religion to soft living and call it "high ghostly thinking." He threw his spud down and darted forward to meet Father Prior. He wanted to tell him that the rose trees had come, with the compliments of the Abbess of Gracerood. There would be roses, roses everywhere against Our Lady's feast. The Father most probably wanted him to pray for some sick wight, or even some sick wight's cow—

Brother Kit was a great medicine man with sick cows, albeit that he was "a garden enclosed," and "a fountain sealed." Or it might be for a sinner? The thought of sinners frightened Brother Kit. "Of all pains, sin is the most deadly," his favourite ghostly guide had said, and thinking on pains gave Kit the pains thought of, which is a sore affliction of the body and, as would follow, of the soul, where the pain be sin.

"Father Prior, the roses——!"

Father Prior had raised his hand for silence. His face was grave. He held the episcopal missive in the other. What could the Bishop's message have to do with him? Could it be that the rose trees were to be sent on to the Bishop's palace? That would be a great act of detachment for Brother Kit. He had so looked forward to seeing the buds come out. But acts of detachment were good for the soul.

"Little son," the Prior said, "I have here a matter which concerneth thee.

Chrysostom was certain then that it must be the roses. But why was his Father so grave? It wouldn't be that Mother Chaffer's cow was dead, for the letter in the Father's hand had the episcopal seal, moreover Mother Chaffer could not letter.

"The Bishop desires thee to receive holy orders," the Prior said, "and that right soon. He hath dispensed thee from waiting until the age when a man may be priested in holy Church."

The other stood, stupefied. He had not so much as entertained a dream of becoming a priest, for even supposing that Our Lady obtained for him the grace of good living, he could never hope to get his tongue round the Latin of the missal. It was indeed the crown of a monk's joy to be able to offer the Holy Sacrifice, but the learning that went with the office was only to be obtained from books, and books more difficult to follow than the sheer Anglo-Saxon of Richard Hampole.

"But, Father," he gasped, "I am but a little praying brother." The Prior continued:

"He wishes thee to take charge of a benefice—one where the sheep are without a shepherd."

"But there be no benefices near about here," Kit objected, "save those that are already served." He wondered if he were listening to a fable—if the Prior would end by smiling and drawing a moral. But the Prior was prodigiously grave.

"Sir Robert Luffkyn, the new lord of Weepingwold, hath a mind to rebuild the church there," the Prior said, "the Bishop can spare none of his clerks, there are too many benefices to fill already. Sir Robert saw thee at the door the other day and was well pleased with thee. He hath obtained the dispensation from the Bishop."

"But—Weepingwold is ever so far away. I should have to leave thee! Thou would not have me leave thee, Father Prior?"

"I would!"

The Prior said it firmly because it was less difficult to be firm. Gentleness would open out a line which would require more resistance.

Brother Chrysostom stood rigid, like a stone image. He gazed out towards the hills. For the time being the everlasting hills were below the sky-line of the tree-fringed slopes beyond which the road stretched to Weepingwold, as many miles as a man might ride in the best part of a day. He had heard of Weepingwold from a youth who had come to Bycross to try his vocation—as God-forsaken a spot, as ever was.

The colour rushed into his face. "But the world is wicked!" little Brother Chrysostom cried. "I shall surely lose my soul. Good Father have pity on me."

He fell on his knees and clasped the monk's scapular.

"Pray to God and not to me," the other told him in husky tones, curiously unlike the Prior's. "Thou wilt surely save the souls of many others." His heart was not without its fear. Suppose the world were to snatch away the soul of Brother Chrysostom and teach him its own songs? He had such a swift ear for music.

Brother Kit let go of the scapular. He knelt upright with closed eyes and devoutly placed hands. Obedience was second nature to him. The other watched him. He watched the tears oozing out from under the lashes on to the little brother's bronzed cheek.

The breeze blew gently from the south. The tallest of the lilies bowed its head towards the motionless figure. Little Brother Kit looked up—suddenly. He was apparently addressing the tall lily.

"Lo, me here, God's servant," he said, very simply; and all the lilies bowed their heads, for the wind was blowing from the south.

The Prior moved away, softly. A weight had been lifted from his soul. His own soul might be called to account for the price he had paid for the renewal of the glories of Bycross, and surely it had been his heart's blood?—but all would be well with little Brother Kit.

The notes of the Angelus bell rang out as he turned and walked slowly back to the cloisters. He cast a backward glance at the garden with the nodding lilies that sent their aroma on the wings of the southern wind across the walls into the wilderness. The words of the Canticle of Canticles came into his mind:

"My Beloved hath gone down into His garden to gather lilies." He smiled, and crossed himself.

.         .         .         .         .

Robert Luffkyn arranged all his undertakings to a nicety. It was typical of his genius that the church house, or rectory, at Weepingwold should have received its roof just about the time that its future occupant received the *corona*, which is the special mark of the clerk in holy orders. The pleasant antithesis of the thatched roof and shaven crown may even have struck Sir Robert's pawky wit. At any rate, when the church house was ready for the parson Tom Plimsett's Kit, with much dure and doleful labour, had mastered enough of the Latin of the Missal and the hard sayings of the theological treatises to be judged fit to receive ordination at the hands of the Bishop. The latter had been indulgent. Priests were grievously scarce, and the piety and innocence of the candidate brought forward by the Prior of Bycross had made ample amends for many deficiencies. They were qualities not too often met with in these bad times when men were still reacting against the horrors of war and pestilence.

For the future, carter Plimsett's Kit was to be known as "Sir Christopher." It had been decided to abandon Chrysostom as being unduly hard on the parishioners.

As for little Brother Kit, he knelt in the chapel on the morning of the day when the Bishop was to lay his hands on his head and change him into somebody upon whom Kit would gaze, as from a respectful distance, and prayed for mercy on his soul. How he loved the place! He had prayed here, content to fix his naked intent on God, and to receive the holy Mysteries from the hand of another and worthier. Now, from this day forward, he would receive the sacred Host as from the hands of Christ Himself. But it was hard to realize the stupendous thing. His soul was filled with fear, and too benumbed to have liking in the thought, as every right-minded man should have on such an occasion. His brethren were kneeling there behind him. He loved every one of them. Fraternal charity had never been difficult, and now, this day he was to leave them for ever.

"Lord, I have loved the beauty of Thy house and the place where Thy glory dwelleth." He had said the words so often, as from the depth of his heart, when he was serving Mass. And now he was to say Mass. To *do* the great thing which the priest does, vested with the power of his Lord. Why did men talk of saying Mass rather than of *doing* Mass?

"Take not my life away among the wicked and my soul with sinful men." How he dreaded the wicked men with their hands full of gifts. Now, for the last time, he was washing his hands among the innocent.

He was to say his first Mass, his stupendous first Mass, at his new cure of souls. It had been intended that he should do so here, in the presence of his brethren,—here, in the house that was full of the beauty that he loved, but a peremptory request had come from the patron of the benefice that there might be no undue delay, and it happened that the native of Weepingwold who had been sojourning at Bycross Priory had been recalled to his home and it was well that the new pastor should have him as a guide on the journey. Wat, the young man in question, had thought to enter the monastery, but after his recovery from an exhausting effort to stimulate the state of spiritual fervour by intensive physical exertion, it had been judged wiser to employ him as an outside man. The Lord of the Manor of Weepingwold had now recalled him to his native soil to assist by the labour of his hands in the making of the new Eden.

Weepingwold was to be a model of what an English village should be in this year of enlightenment, fourteen hundred and eighty something. Labourers, artisans, craftsmen, were being marshalled there to engage in the tanning, or in the renovation of Weepingwold Castle, and the erection of cottages for themselves and their families.

It was a sad leave-taking when the community assembled to bid farewell to their only novice. Floss, one of the Prior's mares, a parting gift from the latter (along with a discipline of little cords which Kit had begged to be allowed to keep) was waiting to carry Sir Christopher (how quaint it sounded!) to his destination. Wat, the outside man above referred to, had his own mount and was carrying the parson's modest possessions. Sir Christopher wore his long cassock, and his austerely-shaven head was covered by a hat of approved design. It made him look singularly unlike little Brother Kit. How they would miss him, with his artless ways, and melodious misdemeanours in silence time. Even when silent, Brother Kit would be singing in his heart and it somehow shed brightness over the place.

Brother Paul had presented his novice with a parting gift—a little treatise on Humility—written in his own hand. Humility runs grave risks out in the wicked world, and the boy Kit had a way with him that was passing winning.

Father Prior was blinking away the tears from his eyes, which the reading of many books had rendered somewhat weak. A large contingent of the latter had already reached Bycross from its new patron, and some of them were imprinted. There was no reason to be downcast, but parting with the little brother was hard.

The gate closed on Christopher Plimsett. The monks returned to their respective tasks. It seemed as though Brother Kit, the boy Kit, who as often as not made a mess of the job in hand, had taken away a great chunk of something along with his modest luggage. How they would miss him—the boy Kit.

In his cell the Prior examined afresh the imprinted volumes. They represented an unlimited number of similar works. The printing press was a mighty teacher raised by God to preach to this eager age. He took one up and blinked at the heavy, black lettering. His eyesight was not improving; he must ask Kit to pray for it. Then he remembered that Kit was no longer at hand to ask for favours in that winning way of his. This volume was the first instalment of the price of his ewe-lamb. Little Brother Chrysostom had ridden away to compass the altar of the Lord in the midst of men whose hands were filled with iniquity, and whose right hand contained gifts.

Old Brother Peter, the infirmarian-sacristan, who would now also act as door-keeper, was trying to persuade the even more ancient Brother—I forget his name—to swallow his medicine. The sick brother was adamant. Brother Peter had long since lost the art of cajolery. "I must fetch the boy Kit," he said to himself, and then remembered that the boy Kit was riding away, arrayed in a shovel hat, to his distant cure of souls!

Brother Peter fell to thinking of Holy Innocents' Day, and the game of the boy bishop which the children played on that occasion. It would be Holy Innocents' Day all the year round at Weepingwold? For little Brother Kit was one of those who would never grow up.

The sick brother stretched out a long, lean arm.

"Give me the medicine," he croaked. "The little brother promised that he would come and sing to me if I took my medicine."

"God forgive me," quoth Brother Peter under his breath as he handed the potion to the other.

# Chapter IV

## *Robert Luffkyn's Eden*

THE JOURNEY to Weepingwold took a considerable time, chiefly owing to the difficult riding. Swamps and rough tracts of forest lay between it and Bycross. Christopher's mind was full of the past he was leaving. All the days he could remember had been spent in the care of the good monks. Carter Plimsett had been glad enough to pass the child on when he took to playing games on his own account with his angel guardian. The guardian angel had rather unkindly forsaken his playmate when lessons took the place of games—lessons had always been dolorous, but he had seen to it that he passed the Bishop's test—which was, again rather unkind of Christopher's angel.

Sir Christopher's companion was not calculated to raise his spirits. Wat, the outside man, was telling him such things as he considered suitable for one of his calling concerning his new cure. The Prior's late outside man was a severe moralist. He had tried his vocation as an inside man, but interior things were not for his having. After being discovered by the Prior with his head hanging sideways and a heightened temperature, gazing at nothing, as like a sheep as need be, in a well-intentioned attempt to become an inside man, he had been relegated to the stable. He minded now that he was talking to a holy priest and so shaped his conversation fittingly according to his ideas—as an "outside" man.

Weepingwold, alack! was a sink of iniquity. No man there cared for the rites of Holy Church. The false friars had been there preaching that no man can be made a priest by the mere anointing of him, and that he could be unpriested by committing sin.

Christopher listened, and peeped guiltily into the recesses of his soul. He had so much to live up to as a priest of Holy Church. It would be easy to give scandal to the little ones.

When he had exhausted human delinquencies as a topic, the outside man made gloomy allusion to the origin of the name of Sir Christopher's new cure. The tomb might yet be seen on the wold where the lord of olden times had buried his wife. All around it lay the bodies of those who had died in the great pestilence. They had dug deep pits and buried them by the hundreds.

It was an infirmity of mind in the outside man that he considered weeping and tombs to be appropriate subjects for discussion with a holy man, and they had told him at the monastery that Brother Chrysostom was prodigiously holy. His words had a decidedly depressing effect, producing the glumness associated in the speaker's mind with sanctity.

They were nearing their destination. Floss was picking her way painfully through the thick undergrowth, for they had left the beaten track and were heading for the brow of a low hill. Weepingwold lay in the hollow beyond.

They reached the crest of the hill. The wold stretched out beneath them. A dense forest on one side, a dreary expanse of bare, uncultivated land on the other. At the edge of the former a building could be seen. Wat shook his head gloomily as he pointed it out. *The Travellers' Rest* was a house of no good reputation, though the wife who kept it in these days had not indeed, murder on her soul, as had her predecessor who had been in league with the robbers.

Christopher eyed the sinister building with a shudder. The fringe of the forest crept up towards it. The road to Greathampton ran that way. To the right the wold was scarred by a patch of what appeared to be human habitations, for smoke was ascending from it.

"The church lies beyond yon clump of trees," Christopher's companion said. The pastor gazed eagerly and caught sight of a stout tower. It had no steeple. Christopher had hoped that his church would have a steeple, a finger pointing to Heaven. "The tomb is out yonder,"—he pointed to a speck in the distance. "It be empty now," he added with a sigh, speaking regretfully in the interests of truth, "but,"—more cheerfully—"'tis a tomb right enough; and there be dead men all round.

"The smoke comes from the tannery," he went on. "We shall smell it soon. It be a foul stink, to my mind. There be no stench like tanning unless it be Hell."

Wat began to grow cheerful. He was gratified to have been able to introduce the above-mentioned place into his discourse to the parson. He pointed to the left. "There lies Weepingwold Castle," he said. "It is being built up again in the new fashion. Sir Robert Luffkyn is fain to set up a brood of Luffkyns in the place of de Lessels."

"How many men hath he brought to Weepingwold?" the pastor enquired. He dreaded this imported population of sophisticated townsmen.

Wat considered that fourscore would be stating the case with moderation. They were housed for the present in huts, but later on Weepingwold would possess cottages as it had done in the bygone days. It was to be a land of milk and honey for the workers, and Sir Christopher gathered that it would be the parson's business to persuade them that milk and honey was a more delectable diet than cakes and ale. The imported parishioner was, if possible even more wicked than the native. The parson would have his work cut out.

Sir Christopher looked down upon what Sir Robert Luffkyn had decreed was to be a land of milk and honey. "They do say the new lord will be whitewashing the black sheep to make them white," his companion observed. "And I see no harm in that way of doing it," he added.

"I do. Sooner would I have them black!"

The outside man was plainly disedified by his companion's emphatic rejoinder, and considerably intrigued. They had told him that Sir Christopher was such a spiritual man. Moreover, no one in Weepingwold criticised the methods of the new lord. It led to being pointed out as an undesirable, and it was not found desirable to be an undesirable in the new vale of plenty. Wat could not have told you exactly why.

Christopher's eyes were on his church. Perhaps the man of unmatched benevolence would erect a steeple on his church tower? A finger pointing to Heaven. He ventured to suggest this to his guide.

Wat seemed doubtful. "He do think that this be Heaven," he remarked, and pointed towards the scene of the extensive building operations clustered round the main abomination—the tannery. A malignant eruption of unsightly dwelling-places, of bricks and plaster and other materials met their gaze as they rode into Weepingwold. "Thou wilt smell the tanning in a minute," Wat said, "save that the wind be in the wrong direction." He added this last with some concern. The wind might play them false.

Christopher was tired, depressed, and very hungry. "I call it more like Hell," he said, bluntly.

The allusion cheered the outside man. It showed that the parson had taken heed of his words. He expanded incautiously.

"If the new lord say it be Heaven, it be Heaven," he said, with a chuckle.

They passed the ancient home of the de Lessels glowering down in eminently forgivable disapproval on the piles of bricks and mortar; the church and rectory stood at the far end of what had once been the village. Christopher felt his heart thrill as he looked on the grey building with its unglazed windows. Beyond them he would be saying his first Mass tomorrow morning; and after that the church would be no longer empty. How cold and desolate it looked now. And to think that he—little Kit, could summon the Guest and fill the church with glory! If only the wicked men with their dangerous gifts would keep their distance all might be well.

The new parson's house stood just across the churchyard. Its new thatch gave it a respectable appearance. An elderly woman, stout and not too comely stood on the doorstep waiting to welcome the new arrivals. Behind her lurked the male factotum who would act as the parson's right-hand man both in the church and the rectory. Weepingwold had possessed its parish clerk and churchwardens in the old days, and might do so again in the good times to come. Ned hoped to assume the former office in due course.

The sight of the genial face of Mrs. Agnes framed in the bleak threshold was human and consoling, though a disquieting departure from the monastic tradition. Kit was very, very homesick. There was no getting away from it. He was but twenty, and he had never been away from home. His attendant introduced the new parson, which by the way, is but a contraction of the imposing term, "personage," with due ceremony. Christopher dismounted. He kept his eyes down modestly. He had been repeating the words of the blessing which he would certainly be required to give, over and over to himself lest he should get his tongue into a knot.

The dreaded moment had now arrived.

But Mrs. Agnes, having cast a glance at the tear-stained face of her new pastor, forgot all about blessings, save to reverse the process. "Bless the heart of him, how tired he looks," she cried. "Poor lamb! Grammercy that the supper be on the hob."

And the poor lamb, that was soothly a shepherd, glanced up into the kind face of Mrs. Agnes, whose handsomeness was in the doing, and thought of his mother, the carter's wife. Mrs. Agnes had the same unhooked nose and the same no particular coloured eyes.

He felt his heart warm within him. "God bless thee," he murmured, in husky vernacular.

Fortunately the outside man was helping Ned with the horses so there was no one to be disedified by the little episode.

A few minutes later the parson was seated in solitary state in front of a dish of savoury meats the smell of which reminded him of the story of Jacob and Esau and the filched blessing. Savoury meats were no longer taboo in his diet. Christopher remembered this. The odour was appealing to what the ghostly writers called "the beastly part of a man," but he must not have a false conscience about the rightful use of creatures. He said his grace and set to, trying to fix his mind on the story of Jacob and Esau instead of the savoury meat before him. Some day he might have to make a sermon on it. The direful thought proved a most effective antidote to the satisfactions enjoyed by the "beastly man."

Christopher hastened through his meal. He was anxious to view his church. He had but seen the exterior. He felt better now that he was no longer hungry. The spiced wine had almost gladdened his heart to the task of sermon-making. He rose and peeped cautiously through the doorway. A strong odour of garlic guided him down a stone passage to the kitchen. Sir Christopher waxed bold and went forward.

The large apartment at the end of the passage contained a group seated round a cheerful fire. It was comprised of Mrs. Agnes, Wat, Ned, the factotum, and—as though to make up for the overweening defunctness of the carcase of a pig that hung from the rafters—Blitherbobs, a live kitten of extraordinary vivacity, with personality enough to justify my having said, "people."

Blitherbobs was the first to catch sight of the figure standing shyly in the doorway. He eyed the intruder askance, and never so much as thought of asking for his blessing. He ran a grey eye that was just turning to green over the cassock of the new-comer, gauging its possibilities. A cleric in a cassock can offer more in the way of a lap than a lout in a jerkin. At the sight of the parson Mrs. Agnes sprang to her feet. Wat and the factotum did the same. Christopher was not a little abashed.

"I be disturbing you," he said, blushing, and speaking in the most novice-like fashion, "but I would fain see my church before it be too dark, if so I might have a lanthorn."

The plea, so modestly put, sent Ned off to find the required article. He returned with a rusty lanthorn and conducted Christopher across the wild, untented churchyard. The sheep and other cattle were still grazing there. Up till lately they had been penned at night in the sacred building. In the old days it had been necessary to keep the church locked at night because there had been much that was worth stealing there. No such necessity had existed for over a century.

Ned pressed the heavy oak door with his knee and it opened. A whiff of chill, malodorous air greeted them. The nave as far as the rood screen had obviously been used as a cattle-house. Tufts of wool still lay about on the ground which had only been swept in a perfunctory manner. The sanctuary, beyond the screen, a really fine piece of carved woodwork, had been put into some kind of order. On the altar a pair of tarnished candlesticks had been placed on either side of a crucifix. There was a missal, and that was all.

Christopher stood on the step under the rood-loft gazing at the impoverished place. He had never witnessed such desolation. The parish church that he remembered in his boyhood had been a warm and friendly place, dight with tapestries and furnished with brightly-coloured pictures and images clad in resplendent garments. There had been the blaze of the votive candles before the shrines, and many coloured lights had come through the painted windows that told Bible stories to the unlettered. It had been the home of warmth and light and wonder to the child. The beauties of the priory church had been of a more austere kind, as was fitting, but equally removed from the nakedness of this destitute house of God. He felt his heart fail him.

Ned held the lanthorn aloft. It was nearly dark. There was a linen cloth that Mrs. Agnes had washed, in the vestry, and a chest full of vestments. All would be handy for the morning.

Christopher glanced up above him. A long, blackened chain was hanging there. Attached to it was a blackened object. A receptacle made in the form of a dove with outstretched wings. It was open. It must have hung thus since time immemorial.

Christopher recognised it, with indescribable feelings, as the sacred pyx.

"Aye, that be the pyx," Ned said. He proceeded to cast a bridge over the hundred and fifty odd years that intervened between Sir Christopher and his predecessor.

"My grandfather did tell me when he was a boy how his grandfather did tell him about the parson being taken with the Death when he was in the church saying his Mass; and how he did creep there later from his sick bed and fetch down the pyx from the loft by the very chain that thou see there, and give himself houseling. Some indeed did think that it was to save the Sacred Host from desecration through being left there with none to say Mass that he did so. But anyway they found him lying dead on the step where thou stand'st now and the sacred pyx empty." It had hung there ever since, for Weepingwold had had no curate since that day when half the village lay dead, and half England, it was said.

Christopher stood in thought. "Can thou reach it down to me?" he asked.

Ned fumbled with the chain. It was rusty and refused to act at first. At length, however, the lever worked and the suspended object was in the hands of the man who had succeeded, after many years, the faithful parson of Weepingwold. He held it reverently. It was apparently made of solid silver but the tarnish of over a century and a half had covered the outspread wings and beautifully shaped head. Christopher detached it from the chain.

"Are the sacred vessels ready for use?" he asked, struck by a sudden fear.

"They be tarnished, too," was the reply, "but they be there all ready."

The shadows were thickening in the dark church. Its walls were lined with the altar tombs of the old family. The grave of Sir Hugh de Lessels possessed no monument. He lay under a plain stone in the south transept. The next altar tomb would be that of a Luffkyn making an ostentatious amend for the Luffkyns whose dust lay unhonoured in the churchyard without. Christopher glanced once more at the naked altar. After tomorrow the church would no longer be a place of grim solitude. Its nakedness would be forgotten. Pallid ghosts of the past would be sunned out of existence by the Presence in the sanctuary. It would be a great home-coming.

# Chapter V

## *The House of Bread*

IT WAS LATE into the night. The new parson had possessed himself of a piece of leather and a clout and the chalice and paten stood beside him showing creditable results of his handiwork. He was now at work on the pyx. His eyes were getting heavy over his task, but it was one after his own heart. The silver pyx seemed to defy his best efforts, but Christopher did not despair. The pyx, this silver dove whose wings he was endeavouring to restore to their pristine brightness, was a little Bethlehem, a "House of Bread." Tomorrow it would contain the Bread of angels for the hungry flock. Mrs. Agnes had made a sufficiency of altar breads.

"Lord, I have loved the beauty of Thy house," sang little Brother Kit in his heart—not out loud for someone might hear him. Oh, the rust in the grooved wing! It had been a tiring day for one used to the cloistered life, and the shock of finding his church in such a state of neglect had told on him. How was he to make beautiful that desolate place? How make worthy the place where God's glory was to dwell? A sense of helplessness overcame him.

But the rust was coming off the dove's head. "Lord, I have loved the beauty of Thy house." This was the House of Bread, this little silver pyx. If he succeeded in making it shining and speckless, might it not be taken as representing the whole house? If the washing of Peter's feet had made him clean all over, might not the polishing of the pyx be taken for the beautifying of the larger temple? That was a mighty consoling thought. Christopher put more strength into his elbow. His mind worked equally busily. "If the eye be single the body shall be lightsome," said Christopher's guardian angel, who was presumably providing him with reflections. By a single eye is meant a naked intent to please God.

There was not so much as a particle of rust left in the crevice of the dove's beak. Christopher had accomplished his task. He was direfully sleepy and exhausted, and he had to be up betimes tomorrow to say his Mass. His first Mass! There would be no bell to waken him. Master Richard of Hampole had written that:—failing a bell let the cock be thy bell, and failing the cock, let the love of God awaken thee. Little Brother Kit devoutly hoped that the love of God would serve him in good stead, for he was very, very sleepy. His candle was burning to the socket and he had not yet said his night prayers.

He knelt down, placed his elbows on the seat of his chair and buried his head in his hands. The candle spluttered, and Christopher's head sank lower. His "eye" was lightsome, but his body was very heavy: he seemed to be slipping out of it.

He was dreaming that he was building a great cathedral with a spire like that of Salisbury out of the materials that lay strewn about Weepingwold, and all the while he was simply polishing the silver pyx.

.    .    .    .    .

The outside man rose from his litter of straw in the adjoining room. He sniffed suspiciously. People who live in wooden houses note the smell of burning. The smell came from the parson's room. Wat hastened thither and peeped in. The candle was spluttering out its last flicker; it threw its farewell ray on a semi-prostrate figure. Sir Christopher was evidently absorbed in prayer. His head rested on the seat of the chair. His body remained motionless. The outside man had heard it whispered at the priory that Brother Chrysostom was uncommon near to the world in which the saints lived, and he had ever longed to witness a saint in ecstasy. More-over, he could now tell the people of Weepingwold that he had seen the wonder for himself. Wat was thrilled to the marrow. He looked closer; there might even be an aureole round the shaven head.

This did not appear to be the case, but there was a round black patch on the centre of the nearly horizontal back which uncurled itself at this moment, and the head of Blitherbobs was reared inter-rogatively. He had found this somewhat sorry substitute for the lap of which he had come in search.

Wat's dream fell about his feet in fragments. Who had ever heard of a saint who had a cat, and a black one at that, asleep on his back whilst that he was in ecstasy? Sir Christopher had merely fallen asleep over his prayers. Wat was disappointed, but withal sympathetic. He had often done the same himself. The candle gave its last flicker. It shone upon the pyx, on the table, as it were setting it on fire. The new parson was but human. He, Wat, would be cau-tious as to what he had to say as to his reputed sanctity.

Blitherbobs tucked his head back into his hind leg and closed his grey-green eyes. The situation had been saved.

.     .     .     .     .

It was assuredly the love of God that woke Christopher next morning. This was the day that the Lord had made for him to re-joice in beyond all others.

He found himself lying on the floor with his head on the fallen cushion of the chair. He had passed the remnant of the night thus. Being accustomed to a hard bed he was none the worse for the experience. He sprang up and strode to the window to greet the dawn. This was the day of his first Mass! He thrust his head out of the window and drank in the fresh morning air. The church was there, just across the ragged churchyard, its door would soon be open for the people to come in and hear Mass, as their fathers had done in the old days.

Ned, who should have been officiating as clerk, was still slumbering. Christopher crept out to the pump for a morning wash, then over to the church. In the morning light it seemed more desolate than ever. The sanctuary proclaimed its nakedness under the cold light from the unglazed east window. The coloured glass had long since disappeared. There was no sign of Ned, but Brother Kit had often acted as sacristan. He was happier doing things for himself.

He penetrated the vestry. The clean linen cloth was there, and a faded but magnificent silk chasuble was spread out in readiness, with the other vestments. It was evidently one that had been kept in preservation through the desolate years in the great oaken press. The sight of the faded, frail vestment set Christopher thinking. It was the mantle of that other parson of Weepingwold. It still retained its original beauty, the gold thread being but slightly tarnished. Christopher's spirits rose. It was a wonderful resurrection. All was going to be well with Weepingwold. He was within a few minutes of saying his first Mass. His brothers would not be there to kiss his anointed fingers, but there would be the people, his flock. Would they realise that it was in sooth his first Mass?

There was still no sign of Ned. He would fain have fetched his own man, Wat, but instinct told him that this might not be the right thing. The new parson was in a novitiate which abounded with superiors, and one girded by rules which were not written handily in a book and the breaking of which might mean something worse than a meal taken on the floor.

It was strange, this loneliness on so great an occasion. Silence was indeed befitting, but it was so hard to kneel down and fix one's mind on Unmade Kind at such a juncture. He whispered the Holy Name, but it was as though he had tapped on a wall instead of striking the strings of a harp.

A few minutes later Ned made his appearance, rubbing his eyes and blinking the sleep out of them.

Was there a bell to summon the people to Mass? There was a bell in the belfry right enough, but it was many a year since anyone had tried to ring it.

Ned conducted the parson to the particularly untidy space under the tower and surveyed the bell rope. One of Farmer Roger's beasts had been a-gnawing of it. Safer to catch hold a little higher up or it might break. Ned stood, softly rubbing his chin and deliberating whilst Christopher caught hold, as high up as he could reach.

The bell above was successfully set in motion. So, also, was the bell-ringer. He was carried high into the air as the rope rose. Ned let go of his chin and caught hold of his garments and the ringer came to no harm. The bell was well in its stride.

"Dong, dong, dong!" it rang out, calling the people to their Mass. For quite a dozen times it sounded its tidings; then, the rope broke.

Christopher stood, hot and exhausted. It was a new way of being lifted up above oneself, this perilous bell-ringing! It was unlikely that the saints had felt like that when they were lifted into mid-air, and they certainly had not come down with soiled hands!

Sir Christopher was surveying his hands in horror. They were blackened and blistered. He must rush away and endeavor to cleanse them before he said Mass. Had he committed sacrilege in using them thus? Ringing the bell was Ned's job, but he had been so busily employed rubbing his chin, and the time was short, and Brother Kit had been so long in the habit of doing anything that came along. Would he ever learn to keep the rule?

Christopher fled through the vestry door to the pump and scrubbed his hands for all he was worth. A few minutes later he was back, vesting himself in all haste. He could hear the sound of shuffling feet in the church beyond. The people were coming up well in answer to his call. That was a comfort.

He peeped through the door into the sanctuary. The lights were on the altar, the server was kneeling in his place. The screen hid the nave from his view but he could hear the congregation moving in the empty space beyond. The great moment had arrived. He sent up his last prayer for assistance and went forth.

He was kneeling on the third step saying the *confiteor*. He was turning now, with downcast eyes, towards the people. Now he had said the *introit*. No, it was not he. He was watching somebody else, a priest of God, saying his Mass. Saying it with surprising ease! It was a wonderful thing to watch a priest as close as this! There was a great, a unique thing, about to take place. His hands—yes, the hands of little Brother Kit—were raised over the bread. He had not to worry about the Latin. This priest was repeating it quite smoothly.

Ned tinkled his little bell. . . . He rang it again. The great moment had arrived. . . .

Now the Priest had become the Victim. And He was communicating little Brother Kit. There were black lines ingrained in his newly-washed hands, and they were bleeding. Kit hardly noticed this. He was murmuring to himself, of the Latin he knew:

*Se dat suis manibus.*

"*Ite missa est.*" Little Brother Kit had finished his first Mass. The parson was facing the people to give them his blessing. This time he raised his eyes to steal a glance at his congregation, who so far had only made its presence known by an occasional shuffle. His eye travelled along the empty nave. Mrs. Agnes knelt there in solitary state. He scanned the naked aisles. Where was his flock?

Then, at the far end, near the door, he caught sight of a huddled herd of sheep which kept itself as close up against the wall as possible, conscious of the fact that it had made a mistake in following its leader through the open door of the erstwhile refuge of Farmer Roger Beakwhistle's flocks. Wat, who had arrived late for Mass through oversleeping himself, had likewise noted the intruders and was busy preparing to drive them out. The frightened creatures fled, helter-skelter, with many a piteous and apologetic bleat which mingled with the words of the last gospel as the new pastor read it, his back once more turned to the congregation.

Mass over, Mrs. Agnes returned swiftly to her dinner pot. The young priest had been somewhat long, but that was to be expected. Sweet King Harry would keep an eye from his high Heaven on her pot that it didn't boil over. Ned slipped off likewise. Wat had vanished at the tail of the scared sheep. In that way he would show his zeal for holy places, the love of them having failed to waken him betimes.

The priest remained before his altar. Had ever a priest felt like this after his first Mass? There had never been a soul to kiss his hand. He looked down at his hands. The skin was broken and there was blood on them. He had scrubbed them so mercilessly. Then he caught sight of his chasuble. The perished silk hung in tatters about the canvas. It had yielded to a touch, like charred paper. It was well that there had only been silly sheep to look upon it. Would he ever say that sublime Gospel at Mass without hearing the piteous bleat of the frightened sheep?

What did it all mean? Who was laughing at him? The angels, for his effrontery? Or the fiends? Or both? No, both could not be doing the same thing. He had enough theology to know that. If the angels were smiling, perhaps the fiends were weeping? Somehow he felt certain that the fiends were weeping. He bent his head. The fact remained that he had said Mass. He was not alone. God forgive him; he had forgotten the Wonder in his heart—and in the pyx.

Mrs. Agnes was becoming anxious about her hot-pot. The young parson was a long time coming to break his fast. He must be feeling hungry. When Sir Christopher arrived, he sat down to his meal with an air of distraction. Mrs. Agnes hovered round, wistful for a compliment as to her cooking. But the parson was paying no attention to the excellence of his meal. He had forgotten all about the "beastly" man and his encroachment, for the moment, being deep in thought. He ate mechanically and at a great pace. "Mrs. Agnes," he said, at length, "dost thou think that the people will come to Mass when they get to know that I am here?"

Mrs. Agnes had her doubts—she might be forgiven, seeing that she had taken infinite pains over that stew.

She shook her head. The ale-house was more in the people's line than the church.

"I rang the bell myself that they might know that there was Mass," Christopher said. He glanced at his hands.

"Well, to think!" Mrs. Agnes said. "I did wonder what thou had been doing with thy hands. 'Tis they that grind the corn and make the bread that soil their hands. Yet," she added in the philosophical way of her kind, "'tis a greater thing that the priest doth that maketh the bread into the Lord's Body."

Christopher went back to church to say Matins. They should have been said before Mass but he had been kept so occupied.

He knelt down in the oak stall against the rood screen. It had been the seat for hearing confessions. He said his Matins. Then he prayed in his own way.

The little silver House of Bread was hanging in its place. What mattered the dank walls. The unadorned altar. The essential beauty of the House of God was unimpaired. The vestment might decay. The moth could destroy the garment, but the Word of God remained. He glanced from the pyx to his hands which had filled it with divinity. They were sore and soiled. As though it had indeed taken hard toil to fill the pyx. The priest of God was indeed a labourer even as those who turned the corn into flour and the grape into wine. The priest who made of the bread and wine the Body and Blood of Christ.

Flail and wine-press. Gethsemane and Calvary—and he the priest with torn and bleeding hands.

There came a sound from the other side of the screen. A man's rough voice was speaking. A strong smell of the tannery assailed his nose.

"Your blessing, father, for I have sinned."

.        .        .        .        .

The penitent had gone on his way. The priest sat on trying to pray. The world was very, very wicked. If only he might put the inside of his head under the pump as he had done his hands! If only he could get rid of this soiled feeling! Sick horror was holding every fibre of his soul. They had told him that the world was wicked, but he had been so innocent—little Brother Kit. But he had exercised another of his priestly functions. He had given God's loving pardon to the sinner.

Flail and wine-press. Gethsemane, and Calvary. Surely a priest must needs understand Gethsemane, where One made Himself sin for our sake? He looked again at his hands. They were soiled as well as torn.

"God's will be done. Glory be to God."

But, the world was very, very wicked.

Then in his ears there seemed to sound the bleating of the frightened sheep, and a sudden pang of pity wrung his heart.

Thanks be to God! Weepingwold had got a shepherd.

# Chapter VI

*Astrotha the Witch*

THE *TRAVELLERS' REST* was a hostelry the evil repute of which had not been exaggerated by the outside man. Mrs. Lyons, its proprietress, however, brewed an excellent ale and Weepingwold foregathered under her roof to discuss matters of local interest. Sometimes there would be a passing guest to join in the conversation and give it a wider scope. At all times there would be the permanent guest upon whom Mrs. Lyons had cast such favourable eyes that his visit had been prolonged indefinitely. Sir Robert Luffkyn's imported population had much to tell the natives. There were not only those engaged in the tannery, but the small army of masons and carpenters who were renovating Weepingwold Castle, or Hall, as it was now called. The fortified parts were being replaced by a mansion which was to rival in style, if not in size, the King's new palace near London. Weepingwold took their stories with a grain of salt. They had travellers' tales to tell, these fellows who had been imported from foreign parts. The yokels listened warily. Glass in every window, forsooth, and numbers of separate apartments, like a pigeon-cote!

The subject under discussion on the present occasion was the new parson, the latest benefaction bestowed on Weepingwold by its new lord. The comments passed were innocuous enough. There was a tendency to make fun of the shaveling who had been placed in office. Weepingwold had been God-forsaken for so long that it felt itself rather like a wight that wears his Sunday clothes on a week day. The only one, however, who had a real grudge against the new curate was Roger Beakwhistle, whose cattle had been housed in the disused church since time immemorial. He had listened to the stories of the incredible elegancies practised up at the castle by the new family without comment. Now that the parson came under discussion he wiped his mouth with great vigour, as business arising out of the statement that towels were used for that purpose by the gentry, and gave his contribution. The seizure of his cattle shelter was a grievance habitually aired by Roger at "the Rest." It being impolitic to direct one's complaints in high quarters, Roger was generally found to be against "clerical aggression." The wan-faced shaveling being the principal aggressor. What did Weepingwold want with a church? The wandering friars who came that way, were good enough for him, and as often as not they had a hard word for the parochial clergy. The friar of the order of the "poor priests" regarded every parish priest as a hypocrite, and Farmer Roger was fain to agree with him seeing that he had been robbed of his cattle house.

"There can be some deal wickedness hidden under a black cassock," he opined. "I have no trust of that which lies within a shaven skull."

The resident traveller—he was a good-natured fellow—gave a facetious twist to the conversation.

"I wonder hath the parson called on the witch yet?" he said. "I am told that he be wishful to know all his sheep by name."

A chill descended on the company at the mere mention of the lady in question. The witch was a fearsome person even to name. She had appeared from nowhere, some little time back, and boldly taken possession of the cell which tradition pointed out as the former home of a hermit of great holiness, and having established herself there, had proceeded to do a thriving trade in forbidden things amongst the yokels. The mention of her name in almost the same breath as the parson's was an indiscretion. The parson had not been informed of the presence of the witch. "He might be thinking that it was a holy hermit that still lived there," the facetious speaker went on. "If there were no one to tell him better. Leastwise, he might get to know that it were a witch if no one told him better—on All Fools Day."

Roger of the scattered flock caught at the inwardness of the remark. Here might be the means of getting even with the parson for the injury done to him. Monday week was All Fools Day, and a merrie jest is always allowable on the first of April. A shaveling may expect such things if he presumes to a cassock and *corona* and sets out to teach his elders—and betters. Roger, it would appear, combined a zeal for the honour of cassock and *corona* with a contempt for the office which it signified. The witch would not fail to cast a spell over the parson, could he be lured to her unholy precincts. Someone had got to be paid off for the sequestration of Roger's vested rights, and the shaveling was a safer person to pay off than his patron. Moreover, it was the person whom the mealy-mouthed called Mrs. Lyons's third husband who had suggested the idea.

·      ·      ·      ·      ·

A voluminous correspondence, as need not be explained, was not one of the harassments of the life of the parson of Weepingwold. The missive which was handed to him by Mrs. Agnes on the morning of the first day of April was the first that he had received. All his messages came verbally, reading and writing being rare accomplishments. The message had been left on the doorstep with a stone to serve as a paper weight. It was sealed and the curiosity of Mrs. Agnes remained unappeased.

It ran as follows:

"The holy hermit that dwelleth in the hollow would fain receive ghostly consolation from the new curate. The same prayeth that the coming of the pastor be kept a privity."

Sir Christopher was thoroughly intrigued. To think that nobody had told him that there was a holy hermit occupying the cell of the famous hermit of old, the same to whom he had ofttimes prayed. The hermit of Weepingwold had been a man of some fame. Like him of Hampole, he had made melody in his prayer. Christopher had wondered if any traces of the cell were left. He had intended to ask Mrs. Agnes, but he had no idea that a successor was actually living there. Why had no one told him? He must ask Mrs. Agnes or Ned. Then he remembered that privacy was enjoined. It was mysterious, but all the same uncommon good hearing. The holy hermit would be dependent on his ministrations. Illness had probably kept him from Mass, unless he had been hearing it privily through the squint. Some solitaries had it that way.

Christopher suppressed the question he was about to put to Mrs. Agnes. No doubt there was a good reason for keeping it private. The world was full of things that were done for good reasons. The ex-novice still accepted many things on faith.

He might have learnt many things from Mrs. Agnes although she herself was not in possession of full particulars. The present inmate of the hermit's cell had appeared on the scene suddenly and shiversomely. Three pack horses—some said they were coal black steeds with fiery eyes—had brought her belongings, and "Astrotha" the witch settled in. In a short time she had established a thriving—"practice" shall we call it? Her uncanny knowledge of the future was only equalled by the efficiency of her potions and her influence over aches and pains—she could equally relieve or produce these—so it was declared—and the latter faculty stood her in good stead against thieves. There was much in her dwelling that was worth stealing for Astrotha believed in creature comforts in a way that her predecessors had never done. She was kept well going with clients—or should I say, patients?—some coming, it was said, from as far as Greathampton itself.

Such was the parishioner upon whose door Kit—it is extraordinarily difficult to call him Sir Christopher—knocked on the morning of the first day of April. He held in his hand a leather bottle filled with holy water, the hermit might surely be in need of some. He knocked very diffidently, in spite of his having received an invitation. He might be disturbing the holy man at his prayers. He would have great stories to tell him about the still holier one who had lived there aforetime. This was a very holy spot.

He gave a start of surprise when the door was opened by a woman. She was a middle-aged woman, of commanding presence, with a fine-featured face deeply pitted by small-pox. In spite of the disfigurement it was a face that men would look at twice.

As for Christopher, he made up his mind that it must be a kind neighbour who had come to clean up for the sick hermit. Holy hermits might accept such administrations from discreet women in times of stress, particularly when they had no good looks to give food for scandal. This poor body had no good looks, at least so thought Brother Kit, looking with compassion on her pitted countenance. "I have called to see the holy hermit that dwelleth here," he explained.

The woman returned his enquiring gaze with interest.

"No one lives here but me," she said. She surveyed his cloth and smiled, not pleasantly, but with some humour. Her voice was rich and vibrant.

Sir Christopher looked puzzled. "They told me that the holy man who lived here wished to see me," he explained. He held out the message. The other scanned it. She was evidently lettered. "Someone has been making a fool of you," she said. "There has been no hermit here for three hundred years."

Kit gazed at her perplexedly. She was dressed in curious, many-coloured garments.

"Thou art not an anchoress," he queried.

This time the other laughed out loud. A hard, if not a harsh laugh.

No, she was not a holy anchoress. She held the door open and with a kind of defiant mockery invited him to enter.

The mockery was lost on Christopher. He was dying to see the inside of the holy hermit's former habitation. He accepted the invitation with alacrity and entered.

The room was certainly not that of a holy recluse. It had been fitted with all the comforts associated with wealth. The atmosphere was heavy with some kind of aromatic scent. A huge black cat, with a bit missing from his left ear, sat before the fire that burned on the hearth.

The parson stood there nervously fingering his leather "bottel," and wishing that he possessed the correct company manners to suit the occasion. He glanced round in silence, thinking of the former occupant and forgetting the company manners. A loom, with some silken skeins, stood in one corner. His hostess followed his gaze. He was thinking of the shabby canopy that hung about his silver dove. "I am a spider," she said, "and I spin webs." She watched the effect of her words with her queer, greenish eyes.

He was looking round again. "It is a very holy place," he said at last. He was thinking of the hermit who had scourged himself gaily to the music in his heart in this very place. His hostess was as little prepared for his answer as she had been for his acceptance of her invitation to enter. Sir Christopher sat himself down and continued to gaze interestedly about him. Someone had made him an April fool, but anyhow, it was well to be seeing the holy hermit's home-place.

"You are looking for my broomstick," the lady suggested. "I stable it outside, tethered to the wall. There, yonder, is my familiar spirit," she pointed to the cat. "They call me Astrotha the witch."

Her visitor smiled at her wit. His embarrassment suddenly disappeared. "I have got a black cat, too," he cried, delightedly. "We call him Blitherbobs. What is thy cat called?"

"I call him Rimmon. He is chancellor of the exchequer of Hades and a knight of the Satanic order of the Fly," was the sinister reply.

Her visitor was really shocked this time. "For shame!" he cried, "to fasten an unclean name on a poor beast that is God's creature as well as thee. Why, it were enough to make one coming across him to do him a mischief!" He patted his knee and Rimmon of the infernal order of the Fly, rose up and appeared to be responding to the invitation.

"If I were thee," little Brother Kit said, as by an inspiration, "I should call her Tibby."

"If you were me," was the prompt retort, "you would be a witch and not a holy priest. Didn't I tell you I was a witch?"

"Nay, thou did tell me that they called thee a witch."

His candid eyes were fixed unflinchingly on her face. There was neither fear nor repulsion in them, nor yet that other thing which she saw in the eyes of others. There was only a certain pity that she should be so disfigured.

And there had been a challenge in his answer. This boy who was impervious to the subtle something which made men forget that "Astrotha" was but a marred beauty had looked deeper still and discovered that which she had almost succeeded in forgetting herself.

He sat there, stroking the cat. He had picked up his leather bottle from the floor by his side and placed it on the table, near to a scroll of parchment, laid there somewhat obtrusively. "'Tis a very holy place," he commented, glancing round him once again. "I brought this blessed water for the hermit, but no doubt thou wilt have need of it, for all that it be such a holy place that thou art dwelling in."

She laughed again, but with less assurance. She was not helping the parson out with his conversation although she was well used to the arts of polite society. Suddenly he caught sight of a lute hanging on the wall. "Shall I sing thee a song?" he enquired, artlessly.

It was hardly a request that a hostess could refuse. He jumped up and fetched the lute. "I used often to sing to the brothers at Bycross," he remarked, "especially those that were sick." He tuned the instrument and struck a chord.

"'Tis a little song of the four winds of Heaven," he said, and started to sing:

> "The minstrel of the golden mouth,
> He felt the wind blow from the south;
> A garden all enclosed he trod
> And sang a song of the love of God.
>
> The good man sent the minstrel forth.
> He felt the wind blow from the north.
> He trod the snow-clad dale and hill
> Singing a song of the good God's will.
>
> He felt the wind blow from the east
> And faced it, like the sacring priest,
> And sang before its blast of ice
> A wonder-song of Sacrifice.
>
> And when the wind blew from the west
> The minstrel laid him down to rest."

The song was finished and the visitor had taken his departure. Astrotha stood gazing grimly at the bottle on the table. Somehow its presence disquieted her. She had drawn her first blank with its donor. She, Astrotha, the maker of potions, of love-philtres! The sight of the scroll somehow displeased her even more. It recalled the scene where Sir Ruthven, the wild knight, the same who had first nick-named her "the witch," had dared her to write certain sacred words backwards, as the necromancers did, and she had done so in sheer wantonness. That wild crew at Castle

Ruthven—men whom she could turn round with her little finger—had dared the matchless Mariquita when she had observed that Robert Luffkyn, the upstart's new paradise lacked a village witch, to set up business there. No village, they said, was complete without a witch—and she had wagered that she would do so and make a living.

One of the gay mob had suggested the hermit's cell as her place of residence, and she had taken up the scornful challenge. She would make an honest living out of the village oafs instead of the lordlings. They believed that the devil was her associate. Fools! She would dare the devil as she had dared them. She had not as yet taken him into partnership. It was easy enough, with a little sagacity, to counterfeit his cunning.

Weepingwold had appealed to her for reasons of her own as the scene of this new escapade. She was satiated with the ordinary adventures of life. She had sampled them all. Robert Luffkyn's paradise could well support a residential witch. She had prophesied to him once, in London, that men would one day come to possess a dozen books to one pair of shoon, and he had been vastly impressed. If his dependents shared his belief in her powers she would have no lack of clients. And so it had proved.

All this passed through Astrotha's mind as she stood there with her eyes fixed on the "leather bottel" which had been the pride of Mrs. Agnes's heart. She had carried the whole thing through. The Lord of Ruthven had lent her his own pack horses to bring her belongings hither. Sir Robert Luffkyn was an object of derision in the set to which the matchless Mariquita belonged. It suited her mood, this new adventure. Or, rather, it had suited her mood up to now. As she stood cogitating on her first failure the joke seemed suddenly to have become a little thin. She was expecting a client shortly, a love-sick swain who was coming to fetch a potion which would induce the lady of his affections to look more favourably on his unwinsome countenance. Poor fools! Her "magic" could do them no more harm than to make them part with their money. Her love philtres were less harmful than other potions in which they would drown their pennies.

This little pastor had found the place holy. The hermit had held his own! In spite of all, it was he who had predominated. But, then, his art was genuine. But surely the priest who had felt his influence was not a prophet or he would have known what manner of woman he was talking to.

The woman who called herself Astrotha paused on that thought. Perhaps he *was* a prophet?

Yes, the hermit's had been the more interesting adventure. His was real, hers was masquerading. She snatched up the parchment roll suddenly and threw it into the embers. Then, with equal ferocity, she seized the bottle. She had it in her hand when, through the open door, she caught sight of her client approaching.

The swain was an oafish fellow. He crept up, with a leer of furtive cunning on his unlovely face. The sight of him sent the witch into a kind of frenzy. He held a coin ready between his finger and thumb, the price of the mixture which the witch had been requested to make up for his complaint. Astrotha glared at him. The joke had suddenly become worse than threadbare. The leather bottle was in her hand. She flung it straight at him, like a ball.

"Wash thy face with that," she cried, "and wash off the ugliness than offendeth thy lady-love."

The clown stooped and picked it up greedily. Then he came forward with the coin. She looked at it and drew back.

"Keep thy money," she said, "that kind loseth its virtue if it be paid for."

The swain went off rejoicing. The fact that the witch's own marred countenance was no advertisement for her wares did not occur to him.

"Bring the bottle back," she called after him, "it belongeth to the parson."

Then she went back into her kitchen, or her salon—whichever a witch's apartment is correctly termed. She looked at her hands, they were wet. The stopper of the bottle had evidently been loose.

Now, holy water must needs be used with faith in order to work its effects. Astrotha had learnt that in her childhood. But then— the faith might have been supplied by the priest who had weened that holy water might serve her need no less than the hermit's.

How many years was it since she had made the sign of the cross? She had acquired a hardy paganism over in central Europe that was not to be met with in England. Astrotha feared neither God nor the devil, or, rather, that had been so up to now. She tried to reckon, rubbing the tip of her moistened finger with her thumb as she did so. Then there was a swift, involuntary movement. The old habit had asserted itself. She had made the sacred sign before which the demons of Hell flee.

Astrotha, the matchless Mariquita, was afraid! The Unknown had her in its grip. Some power outside herself was acting upon her. She had blessed herself—and sprinkled another!—her client.

The little parson was probably at this very moment saying prayers for her, as he had said he would at parting, when he had asked her to pray for him! God help him for a simpleton.

Astrotha overlooked the fact that she had, at this moment, carried out the behest. But she was conscious that the holy hermit was asserting the fact that his cell was a holy place. Like the adventurer in the legend, she was being made to learn that good was stronger than evil.

The black cat jumped on to the table. It rubbed its head against her moistened hand. Like her recent visitor, it had no fear of the witch.

She addressed herself to him.

"Thou art in luck, Rimmon," she said. "Thou hast been exorcised. The parson hath christened thee Tibby."

# Chapter VII

## *The Tomb on the Wold*

CHRISTOPHER was thoroughly intrigued by his visit to the hollow. What manner of woman was this whom the people had nick-named the witch? He had so little experience of people of refinement, and the occupant of the hermit's cell was certainly of the latter class. Someone had played him an April fool. That was evident. Should he tell Mrs. Agnes? It was humiliating to admit that one has been made an April fool, but on the other hand, it was cowardly to shirk humiliations. Christopher resisted the direful temptation to hold his peace and sought his housekeeper in the kitchen and informed her of what had happened directly he got home.

Mrs. Agnes received the information with consternation, mingled with a fiery indignation against the perpetrator of the joke. That the priest should have been lured to the threshold of a woman sold to the devil was sheer sacrilege. Of course, he would not have crossed the threshold.

Christopher blushed. "I went in and sat with her for a matter of ten minutes," he said.

"I trust thou didst reprove her and talk to her straightly of the pains of Hell," was the response, made when Mrs. Agnes had somewhat got over the shock of hearing that the threshold had been crossed.

Christopher's blush deepened. He went hot all over. Never a word of the kind had he said. "I was thinking of the holy hermit that had lived there," he said, "and I sat me down, and—I sang her a song."

The other was petrified into silence. She threw up her hands, and her eyes likewise. The snare of the fowler had captured its prey.

"I did leave her a bottle full of holy water," the culprit said, "and I did ask her to pray for me."

Mrs. Agnes came to attention. She ran her eye quickly over the hooks on the wall where the jugs were kept.

"Was it the leather bottel?" she queried in startled tones.

The parson's guilty affirmative produced a cataclysm which promised to submerge the former one. The leather bottel, and the only one that the rectory boasted, had gone to the witch. It was a perfect one, save that the plug was a trifle loose.

"I will go back now and ask her for it," Christopher said, penitently.

Most assuredly he had been bewitched.

Mrs. Agnes protested. Sooner would she lose a dozen bottles than the parson should place his head again in the lion's jaws.

Terrible stories of Astrotha's evil doings were poured into Christopher's ear. He listened wonderingly.

"It were well," he remarked, at the end of the recital, "that I did leave her the holy water, even though it were in the leather bottel."

Beyond all question the parson had been bewitched!

On the following day there was a development. The leather bottel was returned, by Tom Littlework, the good-for-nothing. He had found it lying on the ground outside the witch's house, and she had called out to him to return it to the parson.

"So much for taking one's pearls and casting them before swine," Mrs. Agnes opined. Moreover, the stopper of the bottle was missing.

"I will go and ask the poor soul if she still hath it," little Sir Kit said, and he looked round for his hat.

Mrs. Agnes was reduced to the calmness of despair. A cork would fit the "bottel" sufficiently well! "Easier to stop the mouth of a bottle than the mouths of the gossips," she commented, epigrammatically, and Tom Littlework was the worst of the lot. He would put it about everywhere that the parson had left his bottle with the witch, presumably for her to fill it.

Sir Christopher ought to have got a fright.

"Maybe she used the holy water before she threw it away," he said, hopefully, the charity which believeth all things strong in his heart. "Be the bottle empty?"

"As empty as a bottle that hath been cast away without a plug need be," was the ironical response.

"All the same," Christopher persisted, "she may have first taken the water." And with the charity which thinketh no evil in his heart he went off to his prayers.

.        .        .        .        .

Christopher had been some weeks now in his new cure of souls. He had got to know some of his sheep by name, but the world was very wicked. He had heard many confessions and he had come to the conclusion that there was but one thing for it—the priest must do penance for his flock. Bob Bolt, who had heard that there was a priest at Weepingwold and who had found no harm in seeking shrift, had been somewhat perplexed in his mind as he walked off. He had not wept—why ever? But the priest had! He had seen him through the screen. Did the priest think that he was going to smite him over the head like the man he had left stark in the ditch? (The man was still stark—hence the confession). One can't be a good-fellow without these things happening in one's cups, and he had never hit a shaven crown, even when in many cups—he, Bob Bolt, was not as other men. The new parson had not as yet learnt the relative nature of virtue, and the moral excellence, comparatively speaking, of Bob the goodfellow.

Christopher had pronounced the holy words of absolution, his second wonder-gift, but what joy is there in giving absolution when there is no contrition in the heart of the recipient? Only the fear of punishment, which, it is true, may obtain pardon. But that love should be defrauded of the sorrow which is contrition—that God's gift of pardon should win no gift of eager love, no rending of the garment which is the expression of the contrite heart, that was a terrible thought to the doomsman who had lived his life in the presence of God. Sin was a terrible thing, but the sinner doing penance made joy in Heaven. "Sin is the worst pain," the anchoress of Norwich had said, and how well he knew that, for the lash was laid about his own soul whenever he heard of the sins of others—*his* others. But sin appeared to be no pain to these sinners who made up his flock of black sheep. He had given each their penance but their hearts remained unrent. They would sin again and again, and receive shrift, for holy Mother Church forgives seventy times seven, whilst the heretics blaspheme her holy patience.

If only he had some quiet place where he might indeed be solitary, he might stand between Almighty God and the sinner and make good. Did he not represent the One who "bore our transgressions?" The hands of the priest were torn and bleeding hands. But he had no facilities for solitude. The rectory seemed to him to be almost without walls. There had been coming and going ever since he had arrived. There had been Sir Robert Luffkyn's bailiff, representing his patron, for Sir Robert was not yet in residence, and contrariwise, a multitude of beggars soliciting alms. Then Mrs. Agnes was a source of constant distraction, seeing that there was no rule of silence in the rectory. She was ever solicitous for his comfort, meaning well, no doubt. Ned was also voluble. It was like living near a waterfall! This constant flow of human speech. Why was the human mind always pouring out its contents instead of being corked up against occasions, like pipes of wine?

It was the outside man who put Christopher on the track of a haven of refuge. He reminded him, as he bade the rectory good-bye, that the tomb on the wold was beyond doubt *the* sight of the village. The thought of the glum monument fitted in with the new parson's mood. He walked out onto the wold and inspected the desolate and deserted place and found in it a solitude after his own heart. The presence of the dead all round kept people from its vicinity. Here was a spot eminently suited to his requirements. Here he might come and pray and lay upon himself the strokes that might win grace for souls. The tomb formed a spacious shelter that would ensure privacy. Here he could take his discipline without the swish, swish thereof searing the heart of the sharp-eared Mrs. Agnes. Nothing escaped the eye or ear of his observant housekeeper. She could deduct a night's vigil from a pale countenance, and had immediately detected the ashes in the leavings on his platter on the day when she had stewed the capon in an extra rich juice.

The way to the wold lay past the tannery, which was in full swing and smelling of nothing describable in these pages. The men at work there were receiving a bountiful wage. Christopher thought of Sodom and Gommorah. Those places might have smelt like Weepingwold *after* they were swallowed up. It was said that Sir Robert Luffkyn's wife was in no hurry to come into residence. She had no great sympathy with his whim of establishing the Luffkyns on the soil. She infinitely preferred the mansion on the banks of the Thames near London. He was confirmed in his dark mood by having witnessed the growing glories of what was to be known as Luffkynwold. He felt certain that, had he looked back willingly on its chimneys he might have deserved to be turned into a pillar of salt, for Luffkynwold was as wicked as Sodom. Scarce one of the men who tanned the leather had appeared at mass, even on Sunday. Those whom he had shriven had not come back on the week day to give thanks for so prodigious a mercy. The world was very wicked.

He approached the tomb, and pulled up, suddenly. A sound of singing, of an exceedingly cheerful nature, broke on his ear. It came from the direction of the sombre erection. Christopher thought of banshees. Then having caught sight of an unmistakably human figure, his mind ran on those who dwell among tombs.

The individual who had attracted his attention was a young man of somewhere about his own age dressed, albeit with a certain carelessness, in the fashion of a townsman. He was seated on a large stone close up to the entrance to the cave, swinging his legs and whistling the stave that the other had attributed to a banshee.

He slipped down on to his feet as he recognised the cloth of the newcomer and was respectful enough in his salutation to dispel the other's doubts as to the nature of his identity. He had a very pleasant countenance, moreover. Keen hazel eyes, and a mouth to which practice had given some agility in smiling. He smiled now in the friendliest manner at Christopher who was himself at the moment a lugubrious-looking object, until the latter brightened up and returned the salutation.

"Well met, Your Reverence," the stranger said. "I trust it hath not given you an ugly shock to find a live man among the dead?"

"I thought that it might be one that was possessed and living among the tombs," Christopher replied, frankly enough. "The Bible telleth of such a one."

"And you took me not for an angel," the other responded, reproachfully. "Yet Holy Writ tells of three angels that sat near a tomb—two inside, and one outside, on a stone, even as I was sitting just now."

"A tomb giveth one to think on death," the parson replied. And he added, being much in the dumps, "of sin, and the wages thereof."

The other waited impatiently to put in his retort.

"But, man alive!" cried he, "can't you see that this is an *empty* tomb? And there be no more joyous symbol to be fashioned than an empty tomb. No man may deny death, but he may go mad and try to forget it; and, lo! he would have his symbol—a banqueting hall built on dead men's bones." He cast his eye over the waste in the direction of the garish new chimney stacks of Luffkynwold Hall. "'Tis a place for men to weep in, and scourge themselves"—his quick eye fixed itself meaningly on something which was protruding from the pocket of Christopher's cassock—"a banqueting hall built on dead men's bones. But an empty tomb! God forgive thee, Sir Parson, for not taking me for an angel, and myself sitting on a stone!"

He paused and regarded the other with a quizzical gravity that demanded an answer.

Christopher was puzzled. Was this, indeed, a witless wight that bandied words? There was so much that gave one to think in what he said.

"But Christ wept at the tomb of Lazarus," he objected, holding his own.

"Aye, and that a minute before Lazarus was to come forth. Soothly He may have wept that men would ever regard a tomb thus, nor ever learn that He was the resurrection and the life, not even after that His own tomb had stood empty."

The speaker had become vehement. Christopher surveyed him, curiously. Where had this strange fellow dropped from?

"Where dost thou come from, sir?" he asked.

The stranger noted the rough country accent and speech. There was a wonderful charm about the simplicity of this country clerk.

"I come from London," he said. "'Tis a city of fine craftsmen who are skilled in the whiting of sepulchres. I had thought that by taking a journey into the country I might perchance find a place where they have removed the bones and eke forgotten to take off the inscription from the covering stone. A change is good for the brain that is hard worked, they say, and I am studying for the Law." He made a grimace. "My father is a judge at the High Courts, and he would fain have it so.

"I have left my horse at yonder inn," he went on. "Think you that I shall find it there, or that there may be verily bones under the *Hic jacet* at the *Travellers' Rest*?"

He broke off and once more glanced at the object which Christopher had been furtively endeavouring to thrust out of sight.

He looked gravely into the other's face.

"Let at it well, Your Reverence," he said. "Justice cries out that no man shall have the best of two worlds. A holy priest is like one that, having been already well served at table, sayeth to him that cometh along with other dishes, 'I thank thee, but I have already been attended to, and that right well.' The bountiful God hath given thee the best of the world which is eternal. Spare a prayer for a luckless wight that may, God wot, be doomed to be Lord Chancellor."

Christopher was silent, doing his best to sum the stranger up. "The Lord might see to it that even a Lord Chancellor did not have the best of two worlds," he said, "so be it that he was a ghostly man that loved not his high estate."

The other's eyes twinkled. "That were well said, Your Reverence. The Lord hath great cunning in making a whip of little cords for those that would fain bear about a discipline. I wish thee luck of this place, but call it not 'Weeping wold,' call it 'Laughing wold,' for it hath a great and mighty jest against the world."

The next moment he had gone on his way. Christopher stood watching him walking off with a swinging stride, his left shoulder carried a little higher than the right. Who might he be? He had not told him his name.

He glanced round him. The desolate place had become transformed. It was Death who lay dead on the misnamed weeping wold. This very human human being who had swung his legs and whistled, had seen to it that in the future, there would always be an angel seated on the stone at the door of the tomb, who would point to the world—to Robert Luffkyn's Eden—as a tomb which had thought to hold its prisoner and failed.

And pain, sorrow, disappointment—what would these mean but that he was getting the best of the better world and it behoved him to come here and bid the solitude rejoice with him.

# Chapter VIII

*The Parson Meets a Personage*

THE PARSON of Weepingwold was sitting at his table engaged in the task of improving his Latin from a tome as ponderous as the title under which he laboured. The parson, as has been already explained, is really an abbreviation of the "personage." It is the duty of a parish priest to be a personage, and Sir Christopher Plimsett was feeling less and less of a personage as the days went by.

The tome contained the works of St. Thomas of Aquin, and in connection with it there had been a disquieting episode a day or two back. A bare-footed friar had called at the rectory, and after being duly entertained, had entered into conversation with "the personage." The discussion had been on the subject of the Summa of St. Thomas, and the friar had been anxious to learn how the parson of Weepingwold regarded a certain point in the intriguing text of the scholastic philosopher. It happened that Christopher had been studying that very page in the Summa, and he had the answer pat on his tongue. The questioner had been reduced to silence and had soon after taken his leave. But judge of the parson's horror when he discovered, on consulting his tome, that the answer he had given had been based on the *per contra* objection quoted at length by the subtle-minded doctor, which, as every scholar knows, is placed before the apologia. The visitor could only have concluded that Sir Christopher was a heretic. Would he report him to the bishop? Was he a spy? The wandering friar might be anybody. Very likely a heretic himself. In that latter case he had been answered according to his folly. He would have liked well the answer. Christopher had smitten his breast as he thought this. God forgive him, he had liked it well himself. Haply it might have been one that was trying to lure him into false thinking? There were so many snares about. In that case his answer might have saved him. He might indeed have hoodwinked the fiend himself. But he could hardly take that consolation to his soul. There had been something very flesh-and-blood about the visitor. Christopher glumly inclined to the notion that he was one who would report him to the bishop as a teacher of false doctrine, and he had, in consequence lived the last few days in a state of nervous tension, trembling lest someone else should come to him with a ghostly problem for solution.

It was thus, feeling very little of a personage, that Christopher was sitting, this damp and dour afternoon, when the door of the rectory was assailed by a loud knocking, followed by a prodigious pealing of the bell.

Mrs. Agnes was out, so was Ned. Christopher was all alone. He sprang up. Beyond doubt the bishop's emissary was here. The heresy laws were in abeyance, but they had burned Sir John Oldcastle less than a hundred years ago. He peeped through the window. There was no sign of a retinue. The visitor appeared to be on foot, whoever it was. A lonely enquirer into the complexities of the writings of the Fathers? The knock was not that of a beggar. It was repeated, certainly not in the manner of a beggar. The parson's mind reverted to the episcopal theory. It must be the bishop's messenger. His horse was probably round the corner.

Christopher pulled himself together. He murmured a *Hail Mary*, and went forth to meet his fate.

He opened the door and peeped out. His gaze was on the level of the face of an ordinary man. He lowered it.

Standing there was a little girl of eight or nine years old. She was cloaked and hooded in a garment which proclaimed her to belong to the gentry. The children of the gentry did not, however, walk abroad by themselves, especially in the wet weather. Who might this be?

He asked this question of the soaked and sodden but by no means dejected figure before him.

A pair of large, grey, purposeful eyes were raised to his as the hood was thrown back to reveal the face inside.

"I am Dame Petronilla de Lessels," the little lady replied. And then she stood watching him, to mark the effect of the announcement.

It was sufficiently gratifying. Christopher looked quite as over-powered as one might expect. It is soothly an astounding thing to be visited by so illustrious a lady as Dame Petronilla de Lessels.

The parson was completely bewildered. He was encountering some extraordinary specimens among his parishioners. This little dame with the illustrious name spoke in the same accent as the one who had called herself the witch. There was something of the latter's commanding manner about her, albeit that she could not be more than nine years old. Although she was shivering with the chill of the damp, and obviously footsore, her manner remained superb.

Where had she come from? Why was she unattended? Dame Petronilla de Lessels explained herself.

"I live with the nuns at Gracerood," she said, "and I have come to you for ghostly counsel on a very important matter."

A certain text in scripture darted into the parson's mind, anent casting stumbling blocks before little ones, but found no hospitality. The main point was to get the child into the warmth. She was a very little one, although her manner gave her more right to be called a personage than the bearer of the abbreviated title.

When Petronilla was seated by the fire she reverted to her business. She wished for ghostly counsel on a *very* important point.

"But the Mother Abbess is well fitted to give thee ghostly counsel," Sir Christopher reminded her, prudently, "unless it be that thou wishest to be shriven from some naughtiness."

Dame Petronilla drew herself up. "'Tis the Abbess that needs to be shriven," she said, "and it be to her that thou must give the ghostly counsel."

She had thrown off her cloak and was standing there, a slight but very upright little figure, the eager face lighted by two very big grey eyes.

"She will not listen when I tell her that I wish to be God in the mystery play of the Garden of Eden."

Sir Christopher received the stupendous utterance with something of a shock. It sounded very Lucifer-like; but there was nothing sinister in the face turned up to his. The eyes had all the attractiveness of guileless childhood.

"But how came thou here?" he asked. "Gracerood is miles and miles away."

"I walked," she said, "and then a good man carried me on his saddle, and then I walked more, ever so much more." She disposed of the question lightly. It was beside the point.

"But why didst thou wish to see me?" Sir Christopher asked. "The Lady Abbess hath her own chaplain and adviser."

Petronilla answered: "Sir John will not do what I ask him. He is afeared of the Mother Abbess. But she ever doth what a priest tells her, and thou must come and tell her that I must take the part of Almighty God in the play. Thou wilt come, wilt thou not?" Petronilla said.

Sir Christopher rumpled the tough fringe of hair round his shaven crown. No wonder Sir John was afeared. Lady Abbesses were awesome folk, as a race, and this particular one was a lady of passing high degree. He pictured himself "telling" the Abbess of Gracerood!

Petronilla continued:

"Joan and Alicia and the others say that I may be Adam or Eve—" she pronounced the names with contempt—"but I would fain be God; or if I may not be God, I would fain be the devil." She fixed her great wistful eyes on the other personage.

Sir Christopher drew in an audible breath at this amazing utterance. "Thou wilt come and tell the Mother that I must be either God or the fiend," Petronilla said, coaxingly, and a small hand was slipped confidingly into his.

"But why not Adam or Eve?" the ghostly counsellor suggested.

It was a feeble effort, but he was new to his task.

Petronilla withdrew her hand.

"Adam was a poltroon that did what Eve told him." There was fine scorn in her tones. "And Eve was greedy!" The scorn was accentuated. "I won't be Adam or Eve."

Sir Christopher deliberated. He might suggest that if Adam was a poltroon and Eve a glutton, the fiend was—a serpent, but that would only be to narrow the issue.

Then inspiration came to his aid.

"How about the angel? The Scriptures say that God set an angel with a sword of flame at the gate of Eden to keep out all that was not holy. Haply the Lady Abbess hath overlooked the angel in the making of her mystery play?"

Petronilla was all attention. She had overlooked the point, likewise.

"How now, little one? Would thou not like to play the part of the angel that was God's own minister with a flaming sword of fire wherewith to keep His garden holy?"

He paused and watched the effect of his words. It was well worth watching.

Dame Petronilla listened and reflected. She was slowly becoming enamoured of the idea. The grey eyes grew bigger and bigger in the strange little face. It really was a wonderful little face. Then it broke into radiance.

Dame Petronilla de Lessels suddenly forgot all about her dignity. She seized hold of the other's cassock. "Come at once," she cried, "and tell Mother Abbess that I am going to be the angel with the flaming sword, and that I am going to slay all the unholy things that creep into God's garden."

Sir Christopher regarded her, thoughtfully. "Pride be one of the unholy things that creep into God's garden," he suggested, improving the occasion. But the insinuation was thrown away.

"Then I will slay pride," the small Petronilla said, gleefully— "with my flaming sword. And lots of other things as well."

Sir Christopher tried again.

"Thou wilt slay the serpent," he said, but this time Dame Petronilla demurred.

"I like snakes," she said, reflectively, "and dogs and cats and horses and weasels. They shall all come into my garden."

Then she added, with a new access of ferocity, "and I will slay anyone who tries to hurt them."

"But it was God's garden," her ghostly friend reminded her. He was passionately in sympathy with her point of view, but it needed revising. "The angel asked Him first who was to be let in or kept out." But his client remained impervious—from the simple fact that she was not listening.

"Adam named the animals in the garden of Eden," she reflected. "I suppose he called the serpent Satan."

Sir Christopher gave it up. He breathed a prayer of thanksgiving that the Mother Abbess of Gracerood had the forming of little Dame Petronilla. She might tackle the incipient heresy contained in an affection for snakes. The pressing question of the moment was how to get the truant back to Gracerood.

He sat watching the child as she devoured the food which he fetched her from the kitchen. What purposeful spirit was this that had faced this adventure in order to achieve the end in view—the bringing of moral suasion on Mother Abbess. What spirit was it that had insisted on playing a leading part? Was it the highest, or the foremost that Petronilla de Lessels took as her vocation? It might be really interesting to find that out from the Mother Abbess, could he but screw up the courage to face that great lady. He had faced two amazing ladies already, Petronilla and the witch. He might hazard a third, albeit that she was a Lady Abbess.

"And you will tell Mother Abbess that I am to be the angel?"

Petronilla de Lessels was riding by the side of her attendant. They had found her a mule and Sir Christopher was mounted on Floss. In a few minutes he would be facing the ordeal of bearding a real Lady Abbess in her lair. True, he was returning the lost sheep and he would be *persona grata* on that account. The Mother Abbess must be in an unthinkable state of anxiety on the child's behalf, she had been absent the whole day. The small dame was in for a scolding. The great lady would have a fine rod in pickle for the delinquent.

Sir Christopher learned all about the play as they rode along. It was to be acted in honour of the king's mother, who was to spend a night at Gracerood on her way from the west. The two little princes would be with her. Hence the importance of the occasion. It would indeed be a pity if they had an Eden without an avenging angel, Sir Christopher opined. The thought of the impending presence of royalty chilled his blood more than ever. Tom Plimsett's son wondered how he was going to behave himself before this high-born Abbess who entertained royalty.

It might have been the king's mother herself who was about to appear to judge by the state in which Christopher found himself as he waited in the parlour. The king's mother was a lady who had much traffic in the making of fit and scholarly priests. 'Twas said that she had endowed more than one college for the training of them. The unclerkly clerk shuddered in his shoes. This Lady Abbess might report on him to the king's mother.

He shut his eyes and said several *Hail Marys* when he heard the sound of footsteps approaching. Then he opened them and was for saying another! The lady who was standing there might so easily have been the one whom he had been addressing. She had slipped in so quietly that she seemed rather to have materialised in the place where she stood, smiling at her visitor.

Petronilla's absence had not been noticed for some hours. The child was given to wandering by herself in the extensive grounds. The Abbess's gratitude was profuse and very charmingly expressed. Petronilla was a strange child. She had strange blood in her veins. Geoffry de Lessels had found his wife in a foreign land. Petronilla was given to playing truant. Sometimes she would take it into her head to play the hermit, and hide away in some corner of the grounds. She had once been out to seek martyrdom—the Mother smiled—a peasant had rescued her from the near approach of a wild boar. The child's dreams were so real to her that she did not seem able to distinguish them from the real things of life. She was always playing at being something, and the something was always of an exalted order.

Christopher listened to all this with a growing sympathy for the mental outlook of the truant. He had already a strong fellow-feeling with the child who would fain invite the dogs and cats and weasels into Paradise. The hard facts of life had seemed to him to be so much more of the stuff that nightmares are made of.

"She hath very great dreams," he ventured to remark (the Abbess was so easy to talk to) "and where there be the most of loveliness there must soothly be the most truth."

The Abbess Hilda was immensely interested in the maker of the shy rejoinder. She loved a human document as the Prior of Bycross loved a parchment. She seldom had time to read the other kind of books. She had heard of this raw youth whom the prior had sent to Weepingwold at the behest of Sir Robert Luffkyn.

"That should be so," she admitted. And then she added, smiling: "Petronilla hath found a champion."

Christopher was not slow to improve the occasion. Now was the time to put in a word for Petronilla's request. His manipulation of the facts of the case did infinite credit to his tact. Petronilla had begged him to put in a plea for her that she might be allowed to play a certain part in the forthcoming play. She had an idea that, being a priest, he might succeed. Christopher blushed to the roots of his hair as he brought out this bumptious remark. She had made her pilgrimage to Weepingwold for this purpose.

The Abbess sat deep in thought. She was so grave that the other thought afresh of the pickled rod. He ventured to continue, the pickled rod had reminded him of the sword of flame.

He expounded his own ingenious way out of the difficulty.

The Mother Abbess listened to the proposed compromise and receded deeper into thought.

He made one more effort.

"Thou wilt not be too hard on the little damsel, good Mother," he ventured. "Thou wilt let her have her part in the play. It be so real to her."

"I was not thinking of the play." The Abbess spoke reflectively. "I was thinking of the great play in which Petronilla will be bound to take her part—the play of Life. It will be ever thus with her. It will either be God or the devil." She darted a glance at the other to see if he took in her meaning. "There will be no mere Adam or Eve possible for her."

Did this open-faced boy grasp her point?

It might be suspected that he did not. His answer was on the lines of the obvious. "There be the angel with the sword of flame," he reminded her, with all due diffidence.

The Abbess smiled. "You have found an ingenious compromise," she said. "Perhaps God will make of her an angel guarding His gate."

Christopher reflected, and decided against warning the Abbess of Petronilla's unorthodox affection for snakes.

"And thou wilt make that same of her, holy Mother, in the play," he said, daringly. He hardly knew himself! Dictating thus to a great lady who associated with the king's mother!

But, after all, Our Blessed Lady was the mother of a King herself, and he was not shy of saying his beads.

"And you will come and see the play," the Abbess said. She had given her assent. She could hardly do less to Petronilla's protector.

"And now, tell me how you find Weepingwold."

Christopher told her. He told her about his first Mass and the empty church, and Farmer Roger's sheep that formed the congregation. And then—yes, he did! He told her of his soiled hands and of that strange thought, that a priest did wound his hands in the saying of Mass. And that he did seem to soil them, in the giving of absolution.

"The world is very, very wicked," little Brother Kit said. "I would fain that thy chaplain gave me shrift before I return, for I have been in the world this four weeks."

She watched him intently. The flush of shame was on his cheek. He was telling her about Bycross now, and how he had been a praying brother. He was never a praying man at Weepingwold. There were so many interruptions. The lady that came to say her little office in church would fetch him away from holy meditation to ask whether it were mortal sin to swallow a gnat in Lent, seeing that insects might be counted flesh. And when he had thought that her mind was at rest she would send again because she had not told him that though the gnat was not swallowed wilfully, the slice of bread that it sat on had been.

The Abbess Hilda came in with her say when Christopher paused.

"But you are no longer Chrysostom, you are Christopher," she said, "and you must shrink not from carrying your burden. And remember that whatever the burden be, it is always the Christ that you carry. And it is the Christ who upholds Christopher even as He weighs him down.

"I will send a singing sister to sing you a song of St. Christopher to while away the dreary time while you eat," she said. "Listen well to the words for they were written by a minstrel that became a monk that had a pretty way with him in telling of the saints. 'Tis called 'The Ferryman's Song.'"

A few minutes later, the parson was seated at table enjoying a double hospitality, of body and soul. From behind a curtained recess came a sound of chords struck on a lute, then there followed a voice singing—a strange, sudden, plaintive cry:

"'Christopher, Christopher! What hast thou done with the Christ?'
    Fair on the hill doth the City stand
    But deep are the waters that water the land,
    And these must be crossed by the pilgrim band—
        Christopher!

    Thou at the ford must vigil keep
    To carry the traveller o'er the deep.
    Still in the night to its brink they creep.

    And many have crossed to the longed-for spot
    Where never hath day the night begot,
    Many yet none, for One comes not,
'Christopher, Christopher! What hast thou done with the Christ?'

    There came not the Christ but a poltroon weak
    Who turned at the ford my aid to seek—
       'Christopher, Christopher!'
    But I said, such as he can cross at will
    Who fears but the lash of the water's chill,
    'Tis his shame that he calls on the ferryman's skill.

    Then he looked on the wave, and he measured its span,
    And he turned from the place where the low tides ran,
    For he got no aid from the ferryman.

    And, said I, it were right that the city fair
    Should be gained but by those who do and dare,
    But a voice rang out and spoiled my prayer;
'Christopher, Christopher! What hast thou done with the Christ?'

## The Shepherd of Weepingwold

Then there came to the ford a worldling wise,
That looked on his scrip with anxious eyes,
And feared for the same should the waters rise.

But I turned at his plea with comfort cold,
And I sent him away to count his gold;
But a voice rang out from the wanderer's wold:
Aye, a voice rang out from the City gate
'Behold, for my feeblest child I wait.
The least of the little ones cometh late.
Christopher, Christopher! What hast thou done with the Christ?'

There came yet no Christ, but a child there came,
There came a child who craved a game.
Who longed for a human steed to ride
On the wonderful way of the flowing tide,
And he clamoured to mount and sit astride,
    'Christopher, Christopher!'

But I said, must I carry him to and fro,
And a child's sport make of the ferryman so?
And I turned on the babe and bade him go.
And he scampered away and was no more seen,
But, far o'er the ford, moved Mary Queen
Seeking her son with the waves between.
'Christopher, Christopher! What hast thou done with the Christ?'

And now to the ferryman come they all
And I bend to the burden, great or small,
By the voice of my Master held in thrall—
      'Christopher!'

And the poltroon stands on the further side,
With never a shock from the shiversome tide,
And every babe has a steed to ride.

And all have passed to the City of light—
All save one—the tardiest wight.
Chiefest of all, I must wait his plight—
    'Christopher!'

So still at the ford my trade I ply,
For many have passed where the waves roll high—
Ninety-and-nine, but the angels cry:
'Christopher, Christopher! What hast thou done with the *Christ*?'"

Sir Christopher was riding homeward. He had bidden farewell to the Lady Abbess of Gracerood, and to Petronilla—the latter reduced to something approaching a penitential frame of mind, had been allowed to come and crave his blessing and pardon for the trouble she had given him by her escapade.

There was soothly nothing to forgive. Gracerood had made him just a little homesick for the garden enclosed, but he was no longer little Brother Kit—he was the giant Christopher. He would dearly love to tell Petronilla that, it would delight her. Held up by the One who weighed him down. He could spend hours over that stupendous thought when humility was the subject of his meditation, that is, if the pious ladies and Mrs. Agnes, and the others would leave him alone. But then—if he were left alone there would most soothly be the voice crying:

"Christopher! Christopher! What hast thou done with the Christ?"

# Chapter IX

## *A Mystery Play, and Exit Astrotha*

THE EPISODE connected with the visit of Dame Petronilla de Lessels served to rehabilitate Sir Christopher in
the eyes of his housekeeper. The parson had acted with
promptitude and discretion worthy of an older head. The Lady Abbess of Gracerood was an ample antidote to the witch. When the
invitation came in due form to the play that was being performed
in the presence of the king's mother, Mrs. Agnes gently allowed
allusions to the cork stopper of the leather bottel to drop out of
her conversation. Sir Christopher was absolved from the penalties
arising out of the regrettable affair.

The performance brought Sir Christopher once more in touch
with the kindred spirit whose champion he had been. It further-
more afforded him an opportunity of serving Petronilla de Lessels
for a second time, although the incident was of so trivial a nature
that it is only with befitting apologies that it is recorded in this
chronicle.

Christopher contemplated the occasion with mixed feelings.
On the one hand he would be delighted to see the "immense little
dame" again whose dreams had the soothfulness of the highest
that one must need love when one sees it. It would be interesting
to see her playing the part which she had chosen, or, rather, which
he had chosen for her. On the other hand, there would be the presence of the royalties. The great lady and her royal grandchildren.
And what was even worse, of Sir Robert Luffkyn and his family.

They had only lately arrived at Luffkynwold Hall, as it was to be called. He had only seen Dame Isabella from afar off, but even at a distance she had filled him with a great awe. The two children, Humphrey and Joan, had looked attractive. As for Sir Robert himself. He had made a hasty inspection of the ex-brother who was half an angel and concluded that he might do, for the time being. Little Brother Kit had never felt more like a pelt, or a pair of shoon, in his life, but the feeling in no sense troubled him.

.        .        .        .        .

When the day arrived, Christopher found himself precipitated into the midst of the distinguished company. He had never been so much as on the fringe of such an assembly in his life, and here he was in the second row, facing the low stage where the play was to be acted —I had nearly said "perpetrated"—by the pupils of Gracerood.

The royal lady was in front, with a grandson on either side. The Luffkyn family came next, on the one side, and the Abbess and sundry persons of importance on the other. Christopher was immediately behind the younger prince.

The little de Lessels dame figured only in the last scene, a kind of epilogue in which Adam and Eve were found wandering in the wilderness, whilst the gate of Eden was guarded against them by the scriptural angel with the flaming sword.

Petronilla stood there, drawn up to her full height—there was a moral six foot of it—holding a very fearsome weapon painted a brilliant red. The younger of the two princes, a fat child who had eaten prodigiously at the foregoing feast, had concentrated his attention on the angel. Petronilla was rejoicing in her *rôle*. She stood, rigid and forbidding—a really terrifying angel. Another spectator, Humphrey Luffkyn, Sir Robert's only son, and heir, was also watching the angel. It had a more arresting face than the damsels who were playing Adam and Eve. For all that she had no lines to speak, the attention seemed to drift towards Petronilla de Lessels.

Humphrey was a silent, observant child. He was calculating what it might feel like to possess a huge pair of wings. He was rather relieved to think that the saints do not share this peculiarity with the other heavenly beings as he had some idea of becoming a saint himself. There was less romance in other avocations. He, nevertheless, took a healthy interest in the sword of flame. His sister Joan was absorbed in mentally commiserating Eve for the ugliness of her desert attire. The latter was delivering a very dull homily on the consequences of being inquisitive, all the moralising being, as it were, congealed in the last act of the play, when there came a welcome diversion.

The fat little prince had noiselessly wriggled out of his seat and was making his way unobserved towards the stage. Cain and Abel having by this time appeared on the scene, the audience scented a murder episode in the near future and fixed its attention on the outer desolation. Not so the fat prince. He approached the avenging angel. The latter remained, stiff and statuesque, guarding Eden. The intruder had his eye on the flaming sword rather than the entry to Paradise. Humphrey Luffkyn nudged his sister and watched. When the prince was quite close up to the angel a fat hand went forth to possess itself of the coveted object.

At that same moment the angel made a swift movement and turned his back suddenly on the audience. It might have been that Cain himself was meditating an onslaught on the forbidden garden. Liberties were sometimes taken with the text of the story, or it might have been that the angel had elected to turn his back on the princeling, but however it was, with the swift turn a feather on the tip of his wing caught the small, fat prince on the tip of the nose.

Humphrey and Joan held their breath. Someone else did the same. Christopher, like the others, was not listening to the sonorous periods of the representative of Eve. He was watching the prince likewise. The latter felt the tip of his nose. It was still there.

Even the skin was intact. Nevertheless, he was obviously contemplating the right-sized yell of pain for the occasion. A most unhappy *contretemps* appeared to be imminent. The angel with the arresting countenance would be getting into fearful trouble if the prince advertised his injury.

The fat small boy suddenly took his hand from his nose, and closed his mouth. He forgot all about the right-sized yell and stared with round eyes at something behind Humphrey. Then his cherublike countenance slowly puckered into a smile. He came back, and kneeling on his seat looked over the back.

In shrill, princely tones he called out:

"Make that funny face again."

Heads were twisted round in all directions, and it was noted that the behest was made to Sir Christopher Plimsett, the new parson of Weeping—no, what was infinitely worse—Luffkynwold.

For the moment the entire two front rows were disorganised.

On the stage, Adam and Eve, Cain and Abel, paused and paid attention to the royal interruption. The avenging angel alone stood rigid, guarding the gate of Eden, with some of the light from the flaming sword transferred to the eyes that were calmly gazing into space.

"I suppose," Joan said to her brother, later on, when the play was over, "when angels don't happen to have a sword they just brush the wicked people away with their wings?"

"There is more power, methinks, in the tip of an angel's wing than in any sword that might be placed in his hand."

The children eyed the speaker. He was a young man with a pleasant face, wearing a scholar's gown. He was one of the guests brought by Sir Robert Luffkyn to view his experiment in the betterment of the people, for he was interested in the subject. "If we were all holy enough to grow wings," he went on, "our Mother the Church, would have no enemies left. But men prefer strapping on swords to growing wings; in sooth, it be the more easily done."

He looked across at Sir Christopher who was standing within earshot.

"*He* be not a holy man," Joan said. "He made a dreadful funny face when Cain was killing poor Abel."

As for Christopher. He certainly was not feeling like a holy man. He had saved the situation for Petronilla, but the Abbess had seen him, and Sir Robert Luffkyn, and quite possibly the king's mother! Little Brother Kit had been a great hand at making faces for the diversion of the brothers who were in danger from the sin of sadness, but that had been in the privity of the monastery where hilarity disports itself at ease, and hath the quality of a virtue. Little Brother Kit should never have been let loose on the world. The world was so very, very well-behaved.

.        .        .        .        .

Astrotha the witch was busy packing up her belongings. She had decided to evacuate the hermit's cell for the time being and return to the haunts of men. Her rustic interlude had proved an undoubted success both financially and artistically, if one may so put it, but quite suddenly she had lost her taste for the escapade which had first proved so entertaining. Astrotha was a daredevil, but she had dared him sufficiently. The evil odour exhaled by the fiend had reached her nostrils. She had won the wager made with the gay lords and squires at Greathampton, and tonight she would accept the invitation of one of the latter who would be paying her a visit to ride back with him to his castle.

Astrotha was not proposing to take her possessions with her. They would be safe enough for the time being packed away in her great oak chest. They included the wonderful oriental apparel in which she sometimes dressed herself in order to impress the yokels. It enhanced the general effect and was a good ally to her natural gift of second sight. There were jewels, too, excellent imitations of the real thing, but there would have been little danger in leaving them, even had they been of value. It was well known that the thief who had been so foolhardy as to break in and steal Astrotha's money had been duly attacked by the mortal pains which afflict a wight whose image is being slowly melted in wax. She took the precaution, however, of affixing a legend to her door, for these that could read to circulate, to the effect Astrotha would return anon. She packed a few things to take away with her, not many. Then she gave thought to her cat. Rimmon of the chivalric order of the Fly had got to be provided for. He could not be left to wander at the mercy of those who would have small mercy on a witch's cat. She had no room for him in her luggage.

The cat sat watching her making her decision, with large, enquiring eyes. He gave a pitiful mew. The sight of her packages had disturbed his peace. Rimmon was every bit as psychic as his mistress.

Astrotha's ready wit came to her assistance. Of all her visitors the little parson had been the only one who was not afraid of "Tibby." He had told her that he had a cat of his own. She made up her mind quickly. Slipping on her cloak she picked the cat up and thrusting him under her arm set forth in the direction of the church.

When she reached the churchyard, Astrotha paused and thought. Rimmon had his big black paws round her neck and was hanging on tightly. Where could she best safely deposit him? She looked over at the rectory. There might be a housekeeper about. A priest's housekeeper could not be expected to take kindly to a witch's cat, unless introduced properly, with no link to its lurid past. There was the church. She noted a tiny window in the sanctuary wall. It was a squint used in former times by the lepers. The opening was large enough to admit Rimmon—Tibby, that was. All the chances were that the benevolent young priest who had sung her a song would be the one to find him in the morning. The poor beast should have as good a chance as she could give him. The best might be hoped for from Blitherbobs' master.

It was soon accomplished. The cat, placed in the deep aperture by his mistress, made good his escape through the slit and disappeared into the church.

Astrotha the witch stood peering in, watching to see what he would do. Tibby had already trotted off on a tour of inspection and disappeared through the rood screen. It was nice and warm in there for the poor creature. She cast a hasty glance round. The squint gave directly on to the sanctuary, and she found her gaze turned full on the altar. She saw the faded silken curtains which veiled the sacred pyx, and the hanging lamp which told of the Presence there. She shrank backward. The matchless Mariquita had excommunicated herself many years ago. She had lived in the parts of Europe where paganism had already begun to rear its head and question the Faith, not as the heretics did, but harking back to the heathenism of the pre-Christian era. In this England, even knaves believed and trembled, along with the devils. It was many a year since she had so much as looked upon an altar. The faded silk of the curtains reminded her of how the parson had eyed her silken skeins and loom wistfully. He had told her that his pyx had need of a new canopy. He had been so amazingly impervious to her spells. So amazingly assured of the power of his own!

Then she found herself thinking: Was He Who was there behind the faded curtains also "impervious"? Was He also seeing no witch, but just a woman who had been merciful to her fellow-creature, the cat? She had been lured hither, and once more the hermit's spell was on her. The air she was inhaling was dank and musty. (There might have been an anker's hold built at one time round this convenient little squint) but as she breathed it there came a sense of vast spaces. Of moorlands and wide horizons. Here was a true land of adventure. She had visited many places, but they were, after all, walled places. She had travelled along so many blind alleys, but this led to open country.

For one brief moment her heart burned with the desire of the everlasting hills. Not so poor a recompense for the mercy shown to one of God's little creatures.

As for the little creature, he found the strange place quite to his liking. Sir Christopher found him curled up on old Mother Hopper's kneeling-cushion next morning with an air of proprietorship which Farmer Roger's sheep had never assumed, even in the days of their undisputed tenure, and Rimmon's future was assured.

Astrotha's exit was made under cover of darkness. The Lord of Ruthven arrived on his black steed and the witch rode away on the pillion which had brought her thither. The matchless Mariquita was a born adventuress. There was an untameable independence about her which made her more difficult of access than others who had dispensed with the protection of a good name. At the *Green Man*, on the outskirts of Greathampton, Astrotha's cavalier pulled up for a draught of good wine. His companion preferred to remain in the saddle—so she said, but when the knight returned it was to find the saddle empty.

Astrotha alias Mariquita, alias other names—she was an incorrigible adventuress—had reached her destination, and doubtless she was grateful enough for the lift. As a matter of fact, there was a written message attached to the saddle in which the late rider thanked the Lord of Ruthven for his very good services and wished him "good-night."

# Chapter X

## *The Parson Entertains a Guest*

IT WAS A GREAT and joyous occasion for the parson of Weepingwold (nobody ever called it Luffkynwold except in Sir Robert's hearing) for he was entertaining a visitor from home. In spite of a whole year having passed, Christopher still thought of Bycross as home. The monks were not supposed to go abroad except under stress of necessity, so the visit was the more unexpected.

It was glorious to see Brother Joseph and receive messages from the others. Father Prior sent his blessing, and Brother Paul—dear Brother Paul!—had sent him another treatise written with his own hand. Brother Joseph smiled widely as he delivered it. Poor old Brother Paul. He loved writing things with his own hand.

Christopher listened greedily to the news of the old place. There were startling things indeed to recount of the changes at Bycross. Brother Joseph sat over the fire on Sir Christopher's hearth and recounted them. Bycross had entered upon a new era of prosperity and usefulness under the auspices of its new patron. The making of books, as Christopher knew, had always been their chief occupation. Now that wonderful new invention, the printing press was to be introduced and books produced by the hundred where formerly there had been one.

Christopher was vaguely disquieted. He resented innovations in his old home. "What will Brother Paul be saying to that?" he queried. The making of books—holy books—by machinery seemed to him to savour of disrespect. Holy books contained holy words—words that might only be written prayerfully and with a bowing of the head.

The brother shrugged his shoulders. Bycross was moving with the times. No other monastic house, save Westminster, had its own printing press. Sir Robert Luffkyn was a great benefactor of holy religion. He had already stocked the prior's shelves with printed books, and soon they would be making their own. This was at present a secret, but "Brother Christopher" might be safely let into it. It would be the business of the monks to overseer the workers who would come along. 'Twas a wonderful man, this Sir Robert Luffkyn, whom the scurrilous wights called "Rob the tanner." But, of course, Sir Christopher knew all about that.

The parson knew well enough. Sir Robert Luffkyn's chimneys sent up their smoke and their odours not three hundred yards away from where they were sitting. Brother Joseph had already made an inspection of the tanning yard and had been duly impressed. 'Twas a great man, Sir Robert Luffkyn. There were scores of strange men working there who spoke the language of townsmen. They lived in the cottages provided for them by the founder of Luffkynwold. He had also viewed the grand new inn, the *Luffkyn Arms* where the sophisticated portion of the community took their refreshment. The natives still favoured the *Travellers' Rest.* The conversation flowed there on less restricted lines. They did not feel, as it were, the shade of the great Sir Robert Luffkyn brooding behind their chairs. The land of milk and honey had made its due impression on Brother Joseph, who was no stick-in-the-mud. He had been willing enough to leave the daily round to ride over with the Prior's blessing to Sir Christopher. The latter was not looking as round and rosy as he had done at Bycross. Being a parish priest apparently did not suit him so well as the cloister, albeit that a man got better fare and no midnight office to break his sleep in a secular charge. His round cheeks had fallen in and grown sallow, and his eyes had a strained look in them that made little Brother Kit look almost grown up! Mrs. Agnes had interrupted them at least six times with trivial messages which no man might interpret as relating to spiritual things. The parson complied with each request, going forth and returning anon. It fidgeted Brother Joseph to desperation. Tom Holt might lack a chisel, but why borrow one of the parson when he was engaged with a visitor? Dickon the witless, had sent in a message that his urgent need was spiritual, but it had turned out to be a new pair of pants and the parson had returned knitting his brow over a fresh problem.

Christopher brightened up considerably when Brother Joseph expressed a wish to see the church. They were amazingly good, the people of Weepingwold. Some day he hoped to have a spire on his church tower to help them to look up for the world around them was very wicked. His poor black sheep were grazing in poisoned pastures, and the diet, so it seemed to appear to their shepherd, had had the discolouring effect on their wool. If only Weepingwold were like it had been in the old times when the corn grew in the fields and men were content to follow the plough and grow bread for their families, and for the altar!

"Hath Sir Robert Luffkyn heard thee say that?" his companion enquired shrewdly. "Have a care. He may be finding a parson that moveth with the times."

"Dost thou think that?" Christopher asked, hopefully.

Nevertheless, he was not a little proud of his church when he took the visitor over to view it. To one accustomed to monastic severity the storehouse of the good people's treasures, for such was the parish church, might have appeared to lack dignity, but in colour and cheerfulness nothing was wanting. The worst patches on the damp walls had been covered with hangings which had obviously started life in other surroundings. What had evidently been an ancestral bed-covering of complicated patchwork draped the pedestal on which stood the statue of Our Lady. The statue itself was a wooden one, with gaily-painted garments, but the Babe in her arms wore a real shirt of silk, destroying the unity of the scheme, but adding to the richness of the ensemble in the eyes of Christopher's sheep. A number of candles were burning before it—a travelling candlemaker had tarried with the parishioners a whole week and made them enough candles to last a year, and then asked nothing for his trouble save the priest's blessing. There were not a few votive offerings in wax, likewise, which showed that Our Lady of Weepingwold was not a stickler for the correct thing in decorative art or she would surely not have granted favours.

St. Mary Magdalen wore a red satin gown which had been presented by Mrs. Lyons of the *Travellers' Rest.* In addition to it she possessed real golden tresses, the gift of a maiden who had bravely walked about the village with her hair bobbed so that she might make the offering!

Brother Joseph was inclined to look askance at St. Mary Magdalen's gown. The ill-fame of the hostess of the *Travellers' Rest* had travelled as far as Bycross. Brother Chrysostom had been such a delicate soul. Had he become coarsened by contact with profane temporalities in which a priest must needs mix himself, however carefully he sets his churchwardens betwixt himself and the money-box?

"I be hoping that 'tis the beginning of her conversion," Christopher said. "'Twas a costly satin cloak that she gave for the making of the gown." He sighed. Mrs. Lyons was a "tardy wight."

"I should have thought that half a dozen strokes of the discipline taken each day for five years had been a surer means of establishing the penitence of Mrs. Lyons," his companion observed, ironically.

Sir Christopher deliberated. "Think thou it would be enough?" he enquired. He was curiously alert to take note of the prescription, but then anything with the stamp of Bycross on it was reliable.

Brother Joseph wondered grimly how Mrs. Lyons' conversion would fare under the penal conditions imposed. After all, there was a golden mean between the presentation of a discarded garment and a penance like this which he had mentioned in jest. But the boy Kit had always had a literal mind.

Great preparations had been made by Mrs. Agnes for the entertainment of the guest. Sir Christopher had been eager to remind her that a monk when seeking alms outside his monastery was at liberty to eat whatever was put before him, and that the most alluring fare might be safely provided for Brother Joseph, into whose way few delicacies came. Mrs. Agnes, thus given her head, made the most of the opportunity. It behooved a host to keep his guest company and the parson would have to take his due share of the repast. Mrs. Agnes chuckled to herself and prepared the savouriest of savoury meats, into which at least a dozen condiments found their way. The rectory table gave her small scope for her culinary skill in the ordinary way.

Now, Brother Joseph was no glutton, thanks to the rule which he lived under. Any man who habitually lives on fish and vegetables may be permitted to smack his lips when he smells roasted meat. You would yourself, reader, so don't be shocked, or begin to imagine that Brother Joseph is going to turn out to be a heretic or a back-slider. The water rose to his mouth as his host said grace—it was almost as long as a monastic one, which was surely overdoing it in a secular rectory. There had been a previous delay for, just before they sat down to table, Sir Kit had invited his guest to inspect the view of the church from the window, and good manners had compelled him to go over and spend at least ten seconds in commenting on the twin gargoyles over against the south transept which Brother Kit thought to be exceedingly funny. He had grown simpler than ever, had little Brother Kit.

The parson was quite as interested in his repast as his guest. And with far less excuse—so Brother Joseph found himself commenting. A rectory was a fine exchange from the monastic cell, from the fleshly point of view. There were two plates filled up and all but overflowing with the culinary triumph of Mrs. Agnes. Sir Christopher started to give a good example to his guest by plunging his spoon into the one set opposite to himself. He fell to, and Brother Joseph did the same.

Of the two it must be confessed that the monk kept it up with the most sustained voracity, although the other protested his appreciation of the fare ever and anon. One might do that, presumably, out in the world. Brother Joseph had cleared his plate long before his host had finished his. He felt himself to be sufficiently well-nourished but his palate was by no means satiated. A fleshly man could go on for ever with such viands before him and no nice feeling about the sin of gluttony.

There was still quite a good amount on his host's plate when Mrs. Agnes appeared on the scene. There was a pedler at the back door that had had his pack stolen by robbers and he was an-hungered. Sir Christopher rose from the table and hastened out, having set down his knife and spoon with the air of a man who has done with them. Left to himself Brother Joseph fell into a soliloquy. That had been an excellent stew. It would be stark cold by the time Kit came back to finish his portion. He evidently feasted well in the ordinary way. The feast had been no exceptional thing for him, yet both portions had been the same size. He eyed the sweetbreads on the other's plate. A mouthful would not be missed. Had it been a monastery, of course the broken meat would have been carried to the beggar, but no doubt beggars were not encouraged in the same way at a rectory. It was a thousand pities that it should waste. He, Brother Joseph, would not be getting a chance of a feast again for many a year. At any rate, a spoonful would not be missed, and it would be good for Kit to have a lesson in the monastic virtue of temperance in eating. He had shown extravagant signs of carnal enjoyment over his meat. Brother Joseph made up his mind. He stretched over and transferred a portion of the helping on the other plate to his own.

"Ugh!" What on earth had he alighted on? An intense bitterness, like gall itself, pervaded his mouth. And, horror of horrors, he had swallowed the noxious morsel. Someone must have been trying to poison the parson. It was devoutly to be hoped that he would not start eating again on his return for it would be necessary to warn him.

At that very moment Sir Christopher reappeared. He sat himself down at the table and, to the consternation of his guest, prepared in a truly carnal manner to eat up what was on his plate.

What was to be done? Brother Joseph was in a quandary. To admit that he had tasted the contents of the other's plate in his absence, would be to confess to the sin of gluttony. Yet, unless he gave the warning, Kit would be poisoned as well as himself. Already he began to feel twinges inside him. It offered a way out of the difficulty.

"If I were thee," Brother Joseph said, "I would eat no more of yon. That which I have partaken of hath given me a grievous pain, almost as though I had been poisoned."

It was truly little Brother Kit who made answer. Tom Plimsett's son.

"Haply it was worth it?" he suggested, cheerfully. "A good helping doth give a pain ofttimes." Wherewith he plunged his spoon defiantly into the mess.

"Stay thy hand!" Brother Joseph shouted. The feeling inside him was increasing in grievousness. "In sooth, I did have a premonition that something was wrong with thy meat and I did taste it to see if it were so, and——" He placed his hands against his waist and gave a deep groan.

The other was looking decidedly uncomfortable. "I did note a bitter taste," he admitted, with evident reluctance, "but have no fear, I am suffering no pains."

"But I have eaten more largely than thou," the brother objected, "thou hadst not the hunger that I had, nor the relish in the meat."

Sir Christopher became more disquieted. "I did note the taste from the beginning," he admitted, "but be consoled, I have no pain in my stomach. Neither would I have thee think that anyone would wish to poison me. That were an evil thought."

But Brother Joseph shook his head. He was by now in screws of agony, and beginning to think of seeking shrift. "There be the farmer whose cattle thou did drive out of the church," he suggested. "Easy enough to slip into the kitchen and pop something into the pot when the cook had her back turned."

Little Brother Kit gave it up. He reddened to the roots of his hair, and looking downward so as not to meet the other's eye, he said:

"Set thyself at ease, brother. I did put the bitter stuff into my plate myself. 'Tis no poison, but only that, being a fleshly man, I have fears of savoury meat. I be not like those that dwell in a monastery and fare hardly. In sooth I would not have told thee this hadst thou not thought that it were poison.

"'Tis but the colic that afflicts thee," he went on. "Wert thou in truth in danger of death it might be well to ease thy mind of anything that may have hurt thy conscience since thy last confession."

Brother Joseph was on his knees. He glanced up at Tom Plimsett's son. The parson of Weepingwold was in readiness to hear more. He smote his chest above the afflicted part. It was true enough the sin of gluttony lay on his conscience. It had been sheer gluttony which had made him help himself from the other's plate. The priest listened. "Thou did put thyself to great incommodity in order to warn me," he said, thoughtfully. "It were painful to self-love to admit that thou had tasted my food."

Brother Joseph smote himself again. "I did lie," he said, "in telling thee that I had an interior knowledge that it had been poisoned. It was from shamefacedness, for gluttony is the most shameful vice in a religious man."

Little Brother Kit meditated on the saying. His eyes fixed themselves on the brother's crucifix. "Nay," he said—it was almost as though he were repeating something that he were reading there—"the most shameful vice in a religious man is that he think himself better than his even-christian."

Brother Joseph smote himself yet a third time. "God have mercy on me a sinner," he said.

. . . . .

Brother Joseph was on his feet again. "The pain be clean gone," he said.

Tom Plimsett's son smiled. "I be right glad of that," he said, "for Mrs. Agnes hath a pancake apiece in the making for us, and if thou wilt I will let thee have the one that hath been let fall in the ashes."

"Blessed be God," quoth Brother Joseph to himself, "for in the making of a saint He hath also made a very perfect gentleman."

. . . . .

It being near Vesper time, Kit went into church and rang the bell to summon those who might like to assist at Evensong. There might be quite a good few. They soon began to appear, some bringing with them the smell of the tannery, others with the smell of the good earth about them. Sir Christopher and Brother Joseph read the psalms between them. It was like old days. The main part of the congregation fingered their beads and took liking in the general delectableness of their surroundings. After Vespers, Brother Joseph took his departure.

Christopher returned to the church after he had seen his guest off. The news he had received about Bycross had been disquieting. It hinted at hurry and stir and bustle, and things which are not done by contemplative men. Sir Robert Luffkyn was indeed a great benefactor to Holy Church, but wherever he went he made a draught and mighty gusts might be blowing through the garden enclosed; and rather from the north than from the south.

The train of thought brought Brother Paul and his prejudices into his mind. There was Brother Paul's gift in his pocket. He had not as yet had time to glance at it. He took it out now. It was a single sheet of parchment upon which was a short piece of writing in Brother Paul's faultless script. It was headed:

*"A Treatise on the Most Holy Name of Jesus."*

It ran as follows:

*"Now the first letter in this Most Holy Name standeth for the Joy that a man feeleth in his heart at the time that he first heareth there the good tidings, and looketh on Eternity and the endless bliss thereof, that be for his having. Then of that shewing followeth Enlightenment whereby he cometh to know himself and the misery of his many sins and grievous offences. And of this enlightenment cometh Sorrow for the thought of the wickedness of his heart and his sin against a so loving Lord. And on sorrow followeth Unction, which be the solace and strengthening of the soul by the Holy Spirit. And from Unction floweth Sweetness.*

*"But haply thou wilt ask: where in all this be Love? And of that I tell thee that Love be soothly in the core and at the summing, for what be Love but meddled sweetness and sorrow?*

*"And so, ghostly friend, thou hast this treatise of the Name of Jesus, as it were to be called out in one breath. Joy, Enlightenment, Sorrow, Unction, Sweetness, which same do spell the Holy Name. And Love be in the core and in the summing.* Amen."

Christopher knelt there with his head buried in his hands. It brought all the old sweetness back to him with a rush. It was so utterly a thing of the Bycross he had loved, this treatise of Brother Paul's. Oh, to be little Brother Kit and to be riding back with Brother Joseph!

In the sanctuary, his portion of the church, the parson's freehold, the silver dove was hanging with outspread, resplendent wings. He, the sower, the reaper, the harvester, who had filled the Heavenly barn with Food, looked up. He thought of his first Mass and of tomorrow's Mass.

A single word escaped his lips. It was the treatise of Brother Paul. Like the Bread from Heaven, it contained in itself all sweetness.

# Chapter XI

## *The Mild Medicine of Master Catus*

"When Weepingwold hath a Luffkyn Lord,
Treasure of gold shall he watch and ward."

SO RAN THE REVISED version of the old adage. It had every appearance of truth in it, for Luffkynwold every day exuded more smoke and odours and became a flourishing industrial centre.

Seven years had passed since its inauguration, but so far Sir Robert Luffkyn had not succeeded in persuading his family to take root in the ancestral soil. The completion of the new mansion gave occasion for a great house-warming which was to emphasise the fact to the surrounding gentry that whereas the Luffkyns had formerly belonged to the soil, the soil now belonged to the Luffkyns. Sir Robert would fain have worked out the *jeu d'esprit* on his armorial bearings—he had, indeed, consulted a Latinist on the subject; it put the whole thing in a nutshell. A heraldic shield, however, it appeared, did possess the same facilities as a nutshell and the matter was allowed to drop.

Sir Robert brought his household down for the house-warming, very much against their wills. Dame Isabella Luffkyn, the serene and matter of fact daughter of a London haberdasher, had her own congenial activities at their manor near London. She suffered Luffkynwold for a space, ever and anon, to humour her husband's whim and fled back to civilisation at the earliest moment. It was the same with Joan, her daughter. Joan, though a lover of the country, loathed the smoke and ugliness of Luffkynwold. She likewise suffered it ungladly, and left the ancestral acres without a pang.

But worst of all was Humphrey, Sir Robert's only son and heir. Humphrey regarded Weepingwold as the abomination of desolation. He had been put to school with the Shene Carthusians, who educated a select number of the rising generation, and had responded to his environment in quite an extraordinary way. His father had placed him there partly to remind the ancient families whose sons were being educated there that the times had changed and Robin the shoemaker was one of the new great, but also for the more practical reason that Humphrey was abnormally bookish—he was hopeless in other ways—and books came into the business proposition in a very definite way. Sir Robert set no great value on learning, but he respected books on account of their covers. In the years to come Humphrey might be placed in charge of the Bycross branch of the leather industry. Sir Robert recognised the essential sameness between the making of a book and the making of a pair of shoon. He was a man far in advance of his times.

So young Humphrey had been encouraged in the study of the "humanities" and even in the acquisition of the new language, Greek. One could not know too much about the different departments of one's trade. He studied greedily, absorbing all that was to be learnt in the famous centre where learned men forgathered, and at the end of the time emerged, that inept and unmarketable thing—a poet.

At Shene, Humphrey fraternised with the choicest spirits of the age which was the opening of a great new era. He read the poems of Petrarch and tried his own hand at a love poem. It was but a qualified success, for Humphrey had but a poor opinion of girls. They had pointed out to him the "mad" navigator from Spain, who had come to England to ask the king to fit him up with a ship in which to travel to the new world which lay in the west. The coming age was to discover a new half to the world. Humphrey had seen the dreaming shipman standing on the banks of the Thames, near the king's palace, gazing across the river with eyes that looked on a vision, and the inadequate love poem he was shaping had changed into an epic, and the Thames into a shoreless sea.

Such was Robert Luffkyn's only son and heir, born to an inheritance of pelts and book-bindings, symbolic of the exterior side of life. And shoon, by the same token! What are one's shoes but the things which we make haste to remove when we stand on holy ground?

It was Robert Luffkyn's custom when he visited Luffkynwold, to send for his bailiff and receive a report of how things were progressing in the land of milk and honey. Weepingwold had been somewhat peremptorily forbidden to weep. Its air of well-being was perhaps a little ostentatious, but duly qualified by the survival of a few of the hovels whose inmates were of the old stock.

John Appleyard's report, when he presented it, was on the whole satisfactory.

Luffkyn consulted his tablets. "Church: Alehouse," he read. It reminded him that the bailiff was to be interrogated on these points. The latter was a mild reproduction of his master. A man of immense gravity, and a certain capacity for putting things through.

Sir Robert embarked on his enquiries. "How goes the parson?" he asked. He had seen but little of the youth who had been pronounced by his superior to be half an angel. Luffkynwold Hall had got its own private chapel and Sir Robert's chaplain would accompany the family in its retinue. The parish church was left to the care of the churchwardens, Luffkyn had no wish to interfere with that healthy tradition. He was anxious, however, to learn something of the curate. He had a recollection of seeing Father Prior's "semi-angel" at an entertainment at Gracerood, behaving uncommonly like a mountebank, or facial contortionist, with no seemly regard for his cloth.

"The parson?" John Appleyard repeated. There was some hesitation in his tones. "He doth well in getting the people to church." The church, it seemed, was crowded on week-days as well as Sundays. Then the hesitation explained itself. The people who heard their Mary Mass before going to work were those who drank their ale at the *Travellers' Rest* rather than at the new *Luffkyn Arms*—the riff-raff, in short. There was indeed a saying abroad that the parson had established his relations with the people who formed his following, by means of an art that he had learnt from the witch who had lived in the hollow. A woman that no honest man would go near.

Sir Robert Luffkyn frowned. "Where is the witch now?" he enquired, in tones suggesting the preliminary step in the removal of refuse.

"The devil hath taken her to himself," John Appleyard replied, stating the fact in his matter-of-fact, monotonous voice. "Some saw him carry her off on a black steed—it was six or seven years ago—and the parson hath her black cat in his house and hath given it the name of Tibby."

It was quite an effective culmination to the harrowing recital. "Beelzebub appeareth to be making war on his own nation," Robert Luffkyn observed drily. "He, perchance, hath taken on the wars of the Barons?" (he never lost an opportunity of having a hit at the barons), "but he hath saved me some trouble if he hath removed the witch. Was she also called Tibby?"

"Nay, she was called Astrotha," the bailiff replied, in his level tones.

Robert Luffkyn became thoughtful. He remained silent, frowning at his tablets. He read "alehouse" there and enquired, somewhat mechanically: "What about the *Travellers' Rest*?"

John Appleyard would have looked graver, had that been a possibility. It was many a year now since a traveller had found poison in his cup at the *Rest*, but much unseemly gossip went on there.

The people who took their refreshment at the *Luffkyn Arms* declared that the parson had a vested interest in the *Travellers' Rest*. He had even held the church ales there when the roof of the church house fell in. Mrs. Lyons had been seen at Mass, but she had yet to be made the true wife of the man who should have been her husband years ago. She had baked the cakes for the church ales, and there had been much frolicking.

The lord of the Weepingwold which had apparently dried its tears so effectively, sat deliberating. There was always danger in the parson frequenting the tavern. A hundred years back it had been necessary to pass an ecclesiastical law forbidding the clergy to disport themselves in such a manner. This young Plimsett was evidently one with the tastes of his forebears. His, Sir Robert's, own chaplain, Sir Amyas de Benham, would never be likely to do such a thing. He must keep an eye on Sir Christopher.

Then he caught sight of something else on his tablets.

"How go things at Graceroود?" he asked. "Hath the Abbess made a nun of the de Lessels damsel yet?"

John Appleyard was not certain. "Some say that Dame Petronilla hath already entered the cloister," he said, "but I know not if it be true. They do say that she hath given the Lady Abbess some trouble in her training, but that she would sooner part with any of her charges than the little de Lessels dame. The damsel will still have it that Weepingwold, I mean Luffkynwold, be her inheritance, and that she is a ward of the Crown, and you her steward." John Appleyard ventured this last statement with some apprehensions. "The Lady Abbess appears to humour her fancy or the child would surely have learnt better ere now."

"She will learn better anon," Sir Robert said, in his dry way. "The maid hath a peacock's pride. She may preen her feathers, if she will, under an Abbess's gown."

He let his tablets fall to his side. John Appleyard had been dismissed.

The *Travellers' Rest*, as might be guessed from John Appleyard's report, had plenty to say concerning the coming festivity at the Castle. There was to be a banquet, and every guest his own knife and fork and spoon. The Bishop had promised his presence and all the gentry from miles round. Afterwards there was to be dancing in the big hall where the banquet had been held, and the finest set of mummers in the country had been hired to divert the company in new and unexpected ways which were to provide a surprise for even the most jaded palates. The *Rest* discussed the whole business at length. Some of its clients might, with luck, be helping in the scullery. Sir Robert's son, whom a member of the company had called a poet, until Mrs. Lyons had warned him sharply against saying such things in connection with the family, was bringing some of the great scholars from London with him. Luffkynwold had become as famous as London itself—it would soon be outstripping Great-hampton as a place of world-wide importance. He was a wonderful man was Sir Robert Luffkyn. And to think that the witless Joe had openly called his son a poet! The mercy was that he had not done so at the *Luffkyn Arms*, where observations were apt to get reported.

As for the poet. He was at that moment making the journey to Luffkynwold in company with his most delectable friend, Master Reginald Catus, M.A., Ph. D., and a great deal more. Catus was perhaps the choicest of all the spirits with whom Humphrey fore-gathered. He was some years older than his friend and had studied on the continent, and become wondrous wise in all manner of things that England was only just beginning to hear about. He carried his learning jauntily, as was the fashion, but there was a rasp in much of his wit that deprived it of true gaiety.

Catus was a typical product of his times. Being the son of one Mr. William Catt, he had adopted the way they had at Rotterdam and called himself Reginaldus Catus. It was a harmless affectation to which great minds condescended. Catus made much sport of the "contemplatives" who insisted on placing the glories of the pagan past behind a "divine cloud of forgetting." He also brought the "unknowing" of the mystic under the lash of his wit. Most people agreed that Master Catus had got a trenchant wit; some, who were also apt to the art of epigram, had opined that a trenchant wit had got Master Catus, and that his principles were the creatures of the pleasantry that presented itself to his alert mind; but this was not entirely fair. Flippancy was rather the cloak worn by one who gave himself to think, and travailed much in the thinking. Humphrey Luffkyn thought all the world of "friend Catus." The idea of inviting him to the backwater where his father had established his enterprise, to take part in the house-warming of the completed Luffkynwold, was a happy thought. Luffkynwold was an experiment which interested everybody with progressive notions. But on the other hand, you had but to scratch Luffkynwold to find Weepingwold. Sir Robert had rebuilt the cottages and made his own dwelling up to date, but the mental level of the natives remained unchanged. The parson, like the church, dated from the period of Weepingwold's first existence. He was at least a hundred and fifty. Friend Catus would revel in the quaintness of his outlook. Then there was Bycross Priory which was well worth a visit. They had a printing press at work there. It was more or less *sub rosa*, but Catus might be let into the secret.

Catus accepted the invitation with alacrity, after ascertaining the fact that Humphrey's sister Joan would be there.

Joan was not in the least modern. She was learned only in the craft of the household, and the making of the simples which her great-grandmother had compiled in the days before the Death— she was, in fact, scarce more lettered than that totally unlettered dame—but Master Catus found her society passing agreeable. The "humanities" had left the master of arts human, after all. In the presence of Mistress Joan, Catus was the merry fellow that nature had intended him to be, with a smile that turned the right way up and a jest that was not itself like a smile turned upside down.

Humphrey and his friend decided to take in a pilgrimage to the shrine of Our Lady of Willesden (I think it was) on their way to their destination. Catus was anxious to make a pilgrimage with the proletariat in order to study human nature. Both young men had been in the habit of making their studies in the class-room, and one may make a study of the proletariat in a class-room without offence to the sense of touch, or hearing or of smell. The crowds that gathered round Our Lady's shrine, touched friend Catus with some roughness, pushing and shoving with the energy of their kind. They addressed one another over wide spaces in raucous tones with enquiries as to the whereabouts of Tom or Jenny, or with facetious comments embodying an elementary form of wit. Catus, his delicately curved mouth drawn down to its most peevish line, took notes detrimental to pilgrimages as an institution. He expressed himself envious of Our Lady of Willesden since the Lollards had declared that she "had a nose and smelt not." A warm disputation with an elderly and mildewed cleric who insisted on calling him "Mr. Catt," on the subject of relics served to put Master Reginaldus thoroughly out of countenance with one of the Church's most ancient devotions.

The aroma of the clients of Our Lady of Willesden was still in his nostrils, and a scathing essay on Pilgrimages shaping in his brain when they rode into Luffkynwold.

"I wonder how the world wags with the little parson," Humphrey remarked. And he proceeded to give Catus some account of the very unsophisticated person whom his father had presented with the benefice.

Catus groaned. "How many relics hath he to exhibit?" he enquired, "and who may his special wonder-worker be?" Then he added: "It might be kind to supply him with one. I wager thee sixpence there would be miracles in Luffkynwold before next Yuletide."

The parson of Luffkynwold was in his church busy erecting a shrine for St. Nicholas, with Ned in attendance rubbing his chin as vigorously as ever over the problems which the parson solved by a more practical manual process, when the sudden appearance of two strangers, gentlemen of quality, caused him to struggle to his feet and remove three nails from his mouth.

The flight of seven years had left Christopher very much the same. He still served others and ran his own errands, although he could boast now-a-days of an army of willing workers less futile than his left-hand man. He loved to do humble things with the hands consecrated to the one great Work.

The new-comers were evidently of that awe-inspiring class, the scholars. Scholars could be worse than Abbesses. He had lost his fear of the latter to some extent since the Abbess of Gracerood had mothered him, but he still retained a guilty fear of scholars. The visitors however, proved to be far from affrighting. The one who introduced himself as Humphrey Luffkyn was a simple, kindly young man, with easy unaffected manners. He reminded Christopher in a way of that other young man whom he had encountered years ago at the tomb on the wold, from whom he had received a "gospel." The other visitor had a pale, intellectual face. Christopher felt sorry for him. He looked as though he might be suffering from the pains inside, which can torture the soul as well as the body.

The visitors suffered being shown round the church with a remarkably good grace. Christopher was forgivably proud of it. There were no less than six images. Humphrey expressed great interest in the dragon which St. George was slaying with a spear upon which no great demands were made, seeing that the dragon was but a flimsy creature; Joe the tanner had made it out of an old pelt. It should rightly have had scales instead of hair but Joe the tanner had taken an artist's licence with natural history.

Master Catus was casting his eyes round the church. Humphrey wondered what was coming.

"You have not here an image of the holy Abbot, St. Valarius," he observed.

Christopher had never so much as heard of the Abbot Valarius.

"No? You astonish me!" Master Catus said. "That is extraordinary—yet, perhaps, not so. The cultus of the holy Abbot is at present but a local one." The saint was a wonder-worker and had wrought many marvels. Haply the parson would like to learn more concerning him? If so, Master Catus would be only too happy to lend him his *obit*. He happened to have it in his possession. Christopher thanked the stranger and accepted the offer eagerly. A new saint was treasure-trove indeed.

"I wager thee sixpence," Catus said to his friend as they rode on their way, "that the cult of St. Valarius will be well established in this parish, and many miracles wrought by him ere many months be passed."

But his friend seemed less inclined to enter into the jest than he.

"Have done with this Abbot Valarius," he said, irritably. "It savours not of loyalty to holy Church to gibe at the saints." His companion flushed. Criticism was one of the things which he found it more delectable to give than to receive.

"'Tis not the saints that I gibe at," he retorted, "but that which people make of them. You would have no use for the mild medicine of a jest."

"Nay," Humphrey said. "Dost thou laugh at the wort that is on my nose, the folks around will soothly laugh at me, however 'tis the wort alone thou dost regard."

But Master Catus was far too much enamoured of his reforming methods to let the joke be. Humphrey himself needed convincing as well as the antediluvian curate. That same night he set himself to compile the *obit* notice of the holy Abbot Valarius, of the famous monastery of Rotterburgh, in the Netherlands. It was a compilation of a highly reminiscent character. Everything that had happened to the most illustrious saints had occurred in the life of the holy Abbot. His miracles were as astounding as they were edifying. Catus read over the result of half a night's labour with considerable satisfaction. The mild medicine of a jest might work much good in the course of time. Nothing serves so well as an object lesson, and cold facts cannot be gainsaid.

Next day Sir Christopher praying in church was fetched back to earth by Ned with tidings that one of the two gentlemen of quality was asking for him. The visitor was in the parlour. Christopher glanced at the screed which was handed to him by Master Catus. It was written on a roll of parchment, in the manner of monastic obits, space being left for the comments on the deceased of the various readers, through whose hands it would pass.

"It appeareth to be like the lives of many saints all in one," the parson said. "I would fain show it to the Abbess of Gracerood, if I might keep it so long?"

Catus was most obliging. It would be a thousand pities not to let the Lady Abbess learn of the devotion. Of course, she must use discretion in mentioning it to the Ordinary as St. Valarius had yet to be canonically recognised. Catus believed (Heaven forgive him!) that his office was already in the making at the Abbey of Dunderhedenburg. Had Sir Christopher never heard of that erudite seat of learning? Impossible!

Kit blushed for his ignorance. The Abbess would probably be better informed.

"Doubtless she will be persuaded to write her comment on the saintly abbot on the roll," Catus suggested. The obit roll would be honoured by having her name at its head.

With that he took his departure. The grease patch on the knee of his velvet breeches, where a small client of Our Lady of Willesden had laid a soiled hand, had been very amply avenged.

# Chapter XII

*Principally Petronilla, but also a Glimpse of Bycross*

THE ABBESS of Gracerood was in her cell applying herself to the econome's accounts. Dame Hilda would sooner have been praying in the chapel but the Vision Splendid waits on the econome's requirements. The last calf purchased had cost eightpence, the one before only four—there came a knock on the door, the inevitable interruption. Dame Hilda tucked the calf away into a corner of her brain and summoned the intruder.

A tall damsel, clad in the sober habit of the cloister, entered. She knelt down as was the custom. The austere garments sat well on the slender figure, and the white veil and coif were an effective setting to the face they framed. Petronilla de Lessels had fulfilled the promise of her childhood. The great, grey eyes, with their long, black lashes, were raised to the other's face. Light and shadow lurked in their depths.

It was evident that Petronilla had something to say of grave import. The Abbess turned towards her. She was making a shrewd guess at Petronilla's business. It was some months now since Robert Luffkyn's ward had made a sudden and characteristically dramatic request to enter the cloister. The Abbess alone had not been taken by surprise. The unexpected was to be expected of Petronilla. That was the trouble with her. She was given to shaping her actions on a large scale. With Petronilla it would be the cloister or the centre of the gay world. The latter was decidedly not without its appeal to her, although how she would fare in it was an open question, for her guardian certainly had no intention of facilitating such a step. The cloister or penury was the choice before Petronilla de Lessels, but she was sublimely unconscious of the fact. Petronilla had clung to the notion that she was a ward of the Crown and that the ancient family property would be hers when she came of age. The unconscionable family pride of the de Lessels seemed to have concentrated itself in the last of the race, with just that touch of exaggeration which made its absurdity self-evident.

It remained for the Abbess to undeceive her, but so far she had not chosen to do so. Petronilla's religious vocation had been a spontaneous growth.

The Mother Abbess had watched the aspirant closely. She had permitted her to assume the habit of the cloister, and thus garbed Petronilla had cast aside the levity of the school-girl, and become a model religious. It now remained for her to make her final decision; and doubtless that decision was the object of the present interview.

It was the child who had refused to be "merely Eve" in the mystery play who now stood before the Abbess. One usually kneels to ask a favour, but Petronilla had apparently forgotten this. She stood there with her head in the air, the demure veil shaken back, rather in the manner of a pony's mane, and made her request.

"Mother, there is to be a great banquet at Weepingwold and I must needs be there for I am now grown-up. I shall need a silken gown and some jewels."

The Abbess Hilda sat scrutinising the maker of this amazing speech. Alack! It was so completely characteristic of Petronilla. When she spoke she spoke very calmly.

"So thou art tired of being a nun, Petronilla?" she said.

"No, no, holy mother!" Petronilla disclaimed the idea with vehemence. "But I would fain go to this banquet ere I leave the world. I am now grown-up. Thou didst say so thyself when thou didst give me the holy habit."

The mother considered the quaintly ungrown-up speech.

"It is not usual for a religious to cast aside her holy habit and don a silken gown," she observed.

Petronilla reviewed this aspect of the case. In order to do so with greater facility she pushed up the white band on her forehead, revealing stray locks of softly curling hair.

"It is only for this once," she explained. "Afterwards I will return hither and be a nun again."

The other was fain to smile in spite of herself. It was so tragically typical of Petronilla. She looked at the eager face in its dishevelled wrappings. Poor little Petronilla! She had got tired of being dressed up in this wise. She was craving to play a new part in the play of life—one that would involve fine clothes. All through her life she would go on thus, playing parts, or rather, one unvarying part—Petronilla paramount. She must always occupy the centre of the stage. The time had come now that Petronilla must have her real position explained to her. She had missed her opportunity of offering great possessions to Heaven, for that which one believes oneself to possess is a true offering in the sight of God and His angels. To this end the Abbess Hilda had allowed Petronilla to go on believing in a phantom fortune.

She glanced up at the great crucifix which was hanging on the wall. The eyes of the Christ were fixed on the girl with something of a question in them. She would try this last time.

"Look, Petronilla," she said. "Look well at the crucifix and choose now, between a silken gown and a serge habit. Thou may'st make thy choice now, but not later."

Petronilla looked well. She remained silently regarding the figure on the cross. Her wonderful eyes grew wide with vision. The woman watching her clasped her hands and prayed. Now was the opportunity, if Petronilla did but know. Great possessions were still hers to give.

The figure on the cross was watching too.

Petronilla drew in a breath. She turned her shining eyes on the Abbess. "I have chosen," she said. "I will renounce all—all." She drew herself up. "And all the world shall know that I have done it, for ever and ever. I will go to the banquet in a silken gown and jewels and I will tell the world with my own lips that Dame Petronilla de Lessels counts her possessions as dirt for the love of Christ."

She threw out her arms with a dramatic gesture. The veil fell from her head revealing a rich cluster of curls. The other was startled by the sheer compelling beauty of the rapt face. Her mind's eye could supply the garments to match. What a glory they would make of this radiant creature, who was still, after all, but a child play-acting.

Petronilla was continuing: "I will have a blue gown," she cried, "as blue as the sky, and silver veil—and jewels——"

The lady in the patched habit raised her hand. "Cease thy fairytale, Petronilla," she said, sternly. "Sir Robert Luffkyn hath sent me no word of this banquet, and there is no reason why he should wish thee to be present."

She paused in the task which was in front of her. Petronilla filled in the gap. "He deems me yet a child," she said.

"And I also deem thee yet a child."

The Abbess Hilda spoke gently and sadly. She had given herself a respite.

"I made too great haste in giving thee our holy habit. Get thee back to thy playfellows and beg Sister Alys to tell thee the story of Cinderella."

.        .        .        .        .

Sir Christopher Plimsett was wishful for an interview with the Abbess of Gracerood. He was seated in the chapel waiting to be invited into the great lady's presence with the obit roll of the Abbot Valarius bulging in his pocket. In the interim he was hearing some of the nuns' confessions, for their own chaplain was suffering from his chest and the chapel was cold. Christopher loved odd jobs. They were far more blessed in the doing than even ones. The last of his penitents had a question to ask. Christopher, for all that the whole countryside sought his confessional, still went cold when pressed for ghostly counsel by those who spoke the English of the King (who, I presume, had just given up speaking French). There was something vaguely reminiscent in the tones of the voice which was addressing him now. The point in question was this. "Was it permissible for one who had not yet taken the vows of religion to return to the world for a space to set her affairs in order?"

Christopher rubbed up the hair over each of his ears and considered. "'Twould soothly be safer not," he said, at length. "The world be very wicked and it possesseth snares for the unwary. One such might not wish to return to her cloister. Soothly it would have to be a sufficiently good and excellent reason."

"The reason is most good and excellent," was the reply. "It be good for the world to be told, to its face, that there be those that scorn its treasures."

"Soothly," Christopher agreed, "but, remember, my dear sister, that had Jonah first tried to swallow the whale, soothly it would have been his own fault that he did spend three days in the belly of that same strange animal."

With this cryptic piece of advice to digest the client moved away, leaving her ghostly counsellor reminding himself that a whale was not an animal at all, but a fish!

Petronilla had had no luck. She had ignored obedience in the matter of asking Sister Alys to tell her the story of Cinderella, and had sought ghostly counsel from the parson of Weepingwold (Petronilla had not heard it called by its other name) instead, and he had said egregious things about Jonah. On the previous occasion he had been most helpful.

It is at the great epochs in one's life that one stands alone.

Petronilla had every intention of attending the banquet. But how it was to be done she had no notion. One cannot go to a banquet without a silken gown, and to get there one needs some kind of a mount. She stayed on in the chapel and prayed, all unconscious that it was the story of Cinderella that she was presenting to the One who ever listens, and ever understands.

Meanwhile, Sir Christopher had interviewed Dame Hilda and presented her with the parchment roll containing the obit of the wonder-worker. She had promised to peruse it and add her contribution, it was most complimentary of Master Catus to suggest it. Now he was on his way to Bycross. It was a long, long time since he had been back to his old home. Not since the much talked of printing press had been set up. He wished to consult Father Prior as to the propriety of attending the housewarming. As he approached the familiar gate he felt a clutch at his heart. Peace would once more spread her wings over his soul when he crossed the beloved precincts. Alack, there was an air of bustle about the place which made it seem strange and unhomelike. The Prior, in a new habit, conducted him to the scriptorium and showed him the great wooden press, and Christopher saw an entire page of Hilton's *Scale of Perfection* produced, as it were, in the twinkling of an eye! The noise of the machine seemed to penetrate the whole place. Father Prior was as a man obsessed with his book-making. Somehow it all went to Christopher's heart.

Brother Paul, his old teacher who had inculcated accuracy into his soul when copying the Scriptures, was seated on a high stool overseeing the half-dozen young novices who were working the press. Sir Robert had provided the new subjects as he provided everything else. It remained Brother Paul's business to tinkle a bell when work-time was up, and at the time of the Angelus. Between whiles he prayed on his beads, and manfully in his heart, that he might discharge this new task of his old age according to the Master's good pleasure.

Rattle and crash. It went on all day long. Sometimes Brother Paul's head would droop forward and his thoughts would go back to the days when he had copied out Holy Writ. He was thinking of little Brother Kit and how he had made havoc of the sense thereof by leaving out a word, when Father Prior came along in company with a young cleric and beckoned to him to come down from his perch. The young cleric was no other than little Brother Kit himself!

The old man was overjoyed. It was a happy meeting, indeed. Sir Christopher was quite consolingly shocked at the notion of Holy Writ being produced by machinery. Why, were an error such as he had made in the old days made by these new workers it would be multiplied a thousand times ere a man could say Jack Robinson. This rattle-crash, diabolical machine would soothly play tricks with the type. Brother Paul had thought this many a time and prayed against the new terror. His post on the stool was no *sine cure*.

He took Christopher to his own tiny cell ere the latter departed, and showed him the treasure which the Prior allowed him to retain in his keeping. It was the copy of the New Testament upon which he had been engaged when the change came. The M.S. was complete all but the Book of the Apocalypse.

"Some day thou wilt finish it," Christopher said, and the old man's eyes brightened. "I have but little time," he said, "but if God willeth, it may be so."

Then he hurried back to the scriptorium to mount his stool and once more mingle his patient prayers with the clatter of the machines.

The Prior was immensely proud of his ewe-lamb. Stories from Sir Robert Luffkyn's little Eden reached Bycross which brought joy and consolation to the Prior's heart. People were saying that the prayers of the parson always got answered. Sinners craved to hear him preach and were converted by his simple discourses. Weepingwold was producing saints! He prayed that spiritual pride might not enter into the heart of little Brother Kit. "Remember, little son," he said to the latter, "that the saints were ever ingenious in the matter of hiding the favours they received from Heaven, lest some breath of the praise of men should tarnish their good works. There were some, indeed, that practised a pious sleight to that end."

Christopher carried away the words in his heart. He had listened eagerly—so eagerly that he had completely forgotten to mention the holy Abbot Valarius, or to ask the Prior if he had ever heard of that admirable wonder-worker.

# Chapter XIII

## *The House-warming*

O N THE NIGHT of the day before that on which the great banquet was to take place, Petronilla went to bed sorrowful. She dreamt of white horses and of one special steed with a golden saddle that waited on her mounting. The Mother had sent her back to the school-room but Petronilla had no objection to that. She intended to make a dramatic re-entry into the life which she had chosen.

Next morning, Neddy, the white donkey, was seen by Petronilla quietly grazing in the paddock. There was a bit in his mouth, and the reins hung about his neck. There was no golden saddle, but Petronilla loved riding bare-back, and she had not had a gallop since the days before she had assumed the austere demeanour of the cloister. Long before she had connected Neddy with her dream she was on his back. It was well to be a schoolgirl again. Her long, hooded cloak which she was wearing was somewhat in the way, but no matter. Across the paddock she was borne. Then the spirit of adventure captivated the rider. In a few minutes the white "steed" was clear of the abbey precincts. She was out on the wold. Weepingwold lay not so many miles away, and—it was the day of the banquet. Surely it was not chance that had placed this opportunity in her way? The next moment she was reminding herself of sober facts. Alas! she could not present herself at a banquet clad in the simple gown of a child of the cloister. She rode on slowly, with loosened rein. She so longed to face the world and cast its glories in its face.

She could indeed wear dazzling white garments at her clothing, but then there would only be nuns to see her, whose contempt for the world was equal to her own.

She was now approaching the village of Weepingwold, a place she had no desire to be seen in. There was a narrow track leading off from the wider one that she had been following. She turned Neddy's head. He ambled down the path obediently. It led into a hollow. Where was he taking her to?

Suddenly she recalled how in the old days her nurse had told her stories of a certain holy hermit who had once upon a time dwelt in the hollow. A delightful old hermit who sang his prayers and made friends with all the wild animals, and died of the joy of it all. A thought came to her that the holy hermit might have understood her had she told him why she had set her heart on attending the banquet. The hermit who sang songs and laughed in the middle of his prayers (they called it "holy mirth" in *his* case), would surely have entered into the glory of the great Act of Renunciation. But it was too late now to invoke him to move the Mother Abbess's heart in favour of her scheme. A little belated prayer found its way up, none the less.

Neddy, who liked going down hill, proceeded without directions. He trotted along, scenting thistles, possibly, until he pulled up in front of a curious deserted-looking dwelling place nearly smothered in greenery. It was plainly uninhabited. Desolation was written all over it. It must have been here that the hermit dwelt of old!

The donkey had found a paradise of thistles and his rider a new adventure. Petronilla sprang off her mount and, a true daughter of Eve for all that she had once repudiated that insignificant rôle, went up and peeped through the ivy-covered window.

Then she tried the latch of the door. After some pushing it yielded and she went in.

The adventurer stood amazed. This was no hermit's cell. Buried in an accumulation of dust she could make out articles of furniture such as they have in houses. In one corner there was an embroidery frame. In another a large oaken chest.

The rôle of Eve suited Petronilla to a nicety. Without a moment's hesitation she lifted the heavy lid. Then she gazed in astonishment with wide open eyes.

A strong scent of cedar greeted her, and of other preservatives. On the top of a pile of shimmering fabrics there lay a silken garment, soft, shining, diaphanous. Beside it was a small box. Petronilla opened it. What appeared to be gems of priceless value lay there.

She was frankly scared. It was a terrifyingly prompt answer to her half shy prayer. She had never really expected a holy hermit to play the part of a fairy godmother! Kneeling down, she turned the wonderful garments over carefully, still doubting the evidence of her eyes. The question was, were they really hers? Miracles didn't really happen except in the lives of the saints. The hermit must have been very, very holy! Then she caught sight of a thin sheet of ivory, such as is used to write upon. There was a name on it in faint, very faint lettering. "Petronilla de Lessels."

The miracle was complete, and unanswerable.

With shaking fingers which could scarcely accomplish the task Petronilla dressed herself. All the glory of the orient was in the *ensemble* when she had finished. She had no mirror to judge the effect by, but the genius for putting on clothes was hers. She stood, a regal figure in the musty chamber, with the spiders to give her worship. A strange new sensation tingled through her being. Then she covered herself up in her voluminous cloak and drew the hood over her face. She had exchanged her thick shoes for a gorgeous pair of scarlet ones which had been in readiness with the other items. Her cloak was long enough to cover them.

The white donkey had fed to repletion when she emerged from the cell. "Quick, Neddy," she whispered into his ear, "or I shall be late for the banquet."

Petronilla was right. Neddy trotted his best, but when they reached the great gateway of Luffkynwold Hall it was to discover that the guests had already arrived. The feast was in progress. The horses and mules which had brought them hither were standing in rows in the courtyard. The servants were collected in the house attending to the kitchen business. Petronilla was able to slip in unnoticed. She had the advantage of knowing the place which had been her home. There was a space behind the great wheel which worked the portcullis which she intended to use as a dressing-room. Having placed Neddy where his kind were being cared for, she made her way thither. She would leave her cloak there and enter the great hall by means of a passage to which she would get access without having to cross the courtyard. It was all very perfectly planned out.

In the seclusion of the place she had chosen, Petronilla made the final preparations for her first and last appearance in public. Her hands trembled as she arranged the soft, shining veil about her head. She adjusted it in the oriental fashion, throwing one end across her shoulder. The result was the perfection of the subtle art of which she was mistress. Once again she felt the wonder of it all. She was rehearsing how she would stand when the eyes of the brilliant company were on her, in the centre of the hall of feasters. She, the lady of the manor come to tell them that she counted all the things they treasured as dross. The strange sensation of power took hold of her again. What a glorious moment it would be.

Then, suddenly she became conscious that there were eyes fixed on her. In the corner, behind the levers that moved the wheel, a man, ragged and emaciated, was watching her with hunger stricken eyes. Petronilla had never seen such hunger. She had sometimes helped to serve the beggars who came to the abbey, but never had she seen a face like this. The eyes were fixed on her as though mutely craving her pity. Out from the kitchen came the smell of savoury meats. The man was evidently very, very hungry.

She approached him and spoke gently.

"Art thou hungry?" she asked.

There was no audible answer, but the eyes grew hungrier, more wistful. She had never seen such an appealing look on a human face before. Her heart-strings tightened.

"I will bid them bring thee some food at once," she cried. "I am mistress here and they will do what I tell them. Thou shalt have food and a bed." She glanced at his feet. They were bleeding from the roughness of the road.

She darted off on her way. When she was mistress of Weepingwold every beggar should have his fill. But she was only mistress of Weepingwold for one night more. She was about to make the great renunciation.

.        .        .        .        .

Weepingwold, in the palmiest days of its feudal splendour, had not witnessed a more distinguished assembly than that which occupied the tables in the great hall on the occasion of the house-warming. My lord the Bishop was there, on Dame Luffkyn's right, and a number of the nobility and gentry from miles round. Humphrey Luffkyn sat near to his father with his friend Catus opposite. The latter was making the sparkle of his conversation agreeable to Mistress Joan Luffkyn next to whom he was seated.

The moment had arrived for the train of ladies headed by Dame Isabella to retire into the withdrawing-room whilst the tables were cleared, the trestles removed and the hall prepared for dancing. In the interval between the withdrawal of the ladies and the commencement of the clearing away, the jester usually made his appearance, or some other mummer whose antics were more suited to the tail end of the entertainment.

The womenkind having duly disappeared, the signal was given for the minstrels to cease playing. The loving cup was making its last round when all eyes were suddenly directed to a figure approaching along the wide gangway between the two long tables occupied by the guests of a commoner order.

A young girl was advancing unattended. A superb creature, dressed in a curious oriental fashion. The company gazed in wonder. The daring departure from the conventional mode of dress gave added distinction to the queenly figure, for the bearing was that of a queen although the face was that of a girl, almost a child. Who was this? What did it mean? Some new form of diversion that their host had provided for his guests?

The new-comer halted in the centre of the gangway, in front of the high table which accommodated the celebrities. She turned to a serving man who was carrying off a dish of meat, and said something to him. The man set down the dish hastily on the floor, there being no other accommodation handy, and turning round called out, lustily, in the manner of a master of ceremonies:

"I pray silence for the Lady Petronilla de Lessels!"

The silence obtained was unimpeachable. The company gaped in astonishment. Jack the fool among them.

Petronilla cast a swift glance round. There were no ladies present, she noted. Perhaps that was why she had not been included in the invitation? Then she fixed her eyes on Sir Robert Luffkyn and addressed him in crisp, imperious tones that were heard by all.

"There lies a beggar at the gate. I desire that food be sent to him at once."

Her anxiety added to the peremptoriness of the imperious speech.

All eyes were transferred to the face of Sir Robert Luffkyn. He had recognised the child whom he had sent to the Abbess of Gracerood to be trained for the cloister. What on earth was the Abbess about to let her appear like this, dressed in this amazing manner, and comporting herself like a fine lady? And that without so much as consulting his pleasure. Which of his guests had been party to it?

What eyes the girl had! What a poise of the head! The Abbess should pay heavily for this.

Meanwhile Petronilla was waiting for her answer. She was conscious that all eyes were fixed on her, and in those of the youth seated next to her guardian she read worship. A thrill ran through her. The wonder of it!

Sir Robert spoke at last. He pointed to the dish standing on the ground where the flurried serving man had placed it in his anxiety to fulfil the behest of Petronilla de Lessels.

"There is food," he said. "Bear it to the beggar if you will."

She turned once more to the man and spoke to him. Once more he was about to obey her when his master intervened. "Hold." He motioned to the man to set the dish down again. "If thy poor man is to have food, take it to him thyself," he said to Petronilla. He pointed to the dish on the floor. "There it is," he said.

The perplexed spectators had come to the conclusion that it was a diversion planned by the mummers. The flow of good wine had left them with no too acute appreciation of the abnormal; nor were they critical of their host's good taste.

But Humphrey Luffkyn had passed on the loving cup for the most part untasted. He was half out of his seat, but a restraining hand held him. It was that of Sir Christopher. The priest, like his host, had been wondering what Mother Abbess had been about. He had been meditating making his escape from the coming possibly unseemly drolleries, when the antics of Jack the fool had been intercepted by this amazing interlude.

"Let be," he whispered. "Let us see what the little lady will do."

So it had been Petronilla who had consulted him about a temporary return to the world. He had suspected as much. Well, her thoughts were now in the right place, with the poor and needy. *Laus Deo!* It was a great little lady—this.

Humphrey was still on his feet.

"Let be," Christopher repeated. "The little lady will surely win."

Humphrey heard him drawing in his breath as they waited.

Petronilla stood there, indeliberate. She scanned the faces of the serving-men who were waiting to clear the tables. They were immovable. They durst not disobey the order that had gone forth from the head of the table.

This man who had given the order was like the Abbess, he did not realise that she was grown-up. He was making sport of her, as he might of a child. She looked at the dish on the floor. Kings and queens that were saints had fed beggars with their own hands. They had their portraits painted in the act; but they had not suffered insult in the doing of it. The beggar man was very, very hungry, and here was the food, but——

Sir Robert Luffkyn was watching her. What a bearing the girl had! An out-and-out de Lessels. But for his order she would have had the whole assembly at her feet. The child at Gracerood was now a woman. How had she got here? What had the Abbess been thinking of?

Petronilla met his gaze. And that of the youth by his side. Again there swept over her the sense of power. The world was a plaything dangling from her wrist. This time it was not the spiders who were watching her. There were human eyes on all sides, and in the eyes of one there was worship.

Humphrey had slipped out of his seat. Petronilla was standing there alone, the only member of her sex present. It was not seemly. His father must be mad!

He had stepped up to her and was addressing her. He was offering her his arm to conduct her to the room where the ladies were foregathered.

She glanced at the dish on the ground. Then at the proffered arm.

"The ladies have already gone to the solar," Humphrey said. "May I crave the honour of conducting the Lady Petronilla de Lessels thither?"

His chivalry might have chosen the yet more gallant action of picking up the dish, but her need, he told himself, was more urgent than the beggar's.

Petronilla capitulated. She took the proffered arm.

The eyes of the entire company watched them as they passed out of the hall. Jack the fool leapt forward and made three capers along the high table.

Catus leant over to Sir Christopher.

"You were right," he said. "The little dame has gained the day."

But the other shook his head.

Jack the fool had tumbled himself into the seat vacated by Humphrey. The company readjusted itself for a new item in the programme.

Christopher glanced round for a means of escape. The world was very, very wicked!

The whale was waiting with open jaws for Jonah. He must hurry away and get to his prayers. He had appointed himself the henchman of the immense little lady. He would not fail her now.

# Chapter XIV

*The Abbess Says "No"*

HUMPHREY LED his companion through the great vaulted corridor leading to the ladies' quarters. A thought struck him as he did so. Perhaps Dame Petronilla would prefer to wait in the ante-room and join the ladies as they passed through on their way back to the hall? It would not be the correct thing for him to remain with her if she joined the company in the solar.

Dame Petronilla infinitely preferred this latter arrangement. She was immensely interested in her escort. They sat themselves down on a large oak settle and Petronilla took stock of him.

She liked his face. She liked the deference in his manner. This comely youth had no manner of doubt in his mind as to her being grown-up. She gathered the fact that he was the son of the man who acted as her guardian. He was an immense improvement on his father. Petronilla questioned him about himself with the utmost frankness. He proved to be thrillingly interesting.

Humphrey told her all about his life at Shene, where all the most glorious intellects of the new era were to be found. He talked of men who had delved into the treasures of the ancient world and learnt to read the language of dead poets who wrote of love and glorious deeds.

Petronilla listened, with glistening eyes. Then he confessed to her that he was a bit of a poet himself, and that he was engaged on a great epic, in the ancient style, dealing with the adventure of the mystical Spanish shipman who had dreamt of a new world across the sea.

A new world! Petronilla's eyes grew wider. Then would it be a world that had never heard of God and His Church? There was a kind of horror in her eyes now.

It was to bring this new world under the standard of Christ, Humphrey explained to her, that made the Spaniard so eager for its discovery. Petronilla's eyes were curiously like the mystical shipman's as she listened. She was hearing new things. Things which had not penetrated the walls of Gracerood. Yet they were things of good repute.

Now he was telling her about the Italian poet who worshipped a very perfect lady called Beatrice, and asking himself why up to now he had never written a love-poem? Tomorrow he would start a new epic and the Spanish adventurer could wait.

It was Petronilla's turn now to tell him something about herself.

"Thy father doth not understand," she said, "that I am now of age to rule in my own house. I am a ward of the Crown, but when I come of age Weepingwold becometh mine to do as I will with. I think I would fain make thee my steward instead of thy father."

Sir Robert Luffkyn's heir sat dumbfounded. What amazing illusion had this superb creature been allowed to cherish? Was the Mother Abbess mad? Who was going to disillusion her?

Petronilla continued. "When I am mistress of Weepingwold I will fill it with scholars and poets, and grow corn, and turn out all the evil smells." Her eyes shone with delight in the new thought.

She had got the idea so firmly in her head. How was he to save her?

The answer came to him with an intoxicating rush.

"Soothly it will be thine own fault, sweet lady, if some day thou art not mistress of all that is now my father's."

He had dropped on to one knee and was seeking to take her hand.

The lady did not seem displeased. Surely she had grasped his meaning. How delicately he had done it. How gloriously he had solved the problem. Yes, most certainly she understood; and she was not displeased.

Petronilla was not in the least displeased. She overlooked his looseness of diction in alluding to his father's term of tenure. She was thinking, vividly. Yes, it would be "her own fault," the great renunciation. Only for this night was she to be the lady of Weepingwold. He bent and kissed her hand. A little shudder ran through her. It was to be such a mighty renunciation. This morning she had not realised how mighty. The world was so wonderful with its noble purposes, its thinkers and its poets, and its far horizons. There was much to be done in the world by noble-hearted people, like the shipman of Spain.

They heard the rustle of the ladies' skirts as they approached. They were returning to the hall for the great ball. The ball where Petronilla was to shine as a star in order to perfect the setting of her great renunciation. That would come at the end. She was the lady of Weepingwold till then. The lady of Weepingwold who could do so much good in this wonderful new world.

"I will take you to my mother," Humphrey said. "And you must know my sister Joan."

"Is she like you?" Petronilla asked, roused from following a new thought—or possibly assisted in pursuing it.

Humphrey laughed. "Joan cares not for poetry," he said, "and she never dreams; but she feeds all the beggars——"

He checked himself. Petronilla had sprung to her feet.

"The beggar!" she cried. "Oh, the beggar! I had forgotten him."

She was gazing past him now, with pain stricken eyes. "I almost thought I saw him—standing over there," she said, and pointed down the passage that led to the courtyard.

Her great eyes, indeed, seemed to be gazing at a face rather than a memory, but there was no one in sight.

"I will go and look for him and bring him in," Humphrey said. "What was he like? Ragged, of course."

She nodded. The tears rained down her cheeks.

"Old?"

"No, not old."

"And ugly."

"Oh, no! Not ugly. Beautiful. As beautiful as—as the Christ on the cross." Her voice dropped to a whisper. There was a strange, new beauty in her own face.

Before he could prevent her she had darted off down the passage. Humphrey followed. There was a door leading into the courtyard, and others into the various kitchen offices. He stumbled out into the dark. There was no sign of Petronilla. The courtyard was full of horses champing their feed. He waited a while. Then he concluded that she must have remained inside. Perhaps she had gone first to the buttery in search of food? Or by now she might have gone by herself to the ball-room? But the ball-room contained no trace of the vanished lady. Back he fled to the courtyard, into the kitchen offices. No one had seen either the beggar or the lady.

Humphrey stood in the great vaulted passage where they had parted and asked himself the question—had he dreamt Petronilla de Lessels? No, she had been flesh and blood, had not his lips touched the tips of her fingers? She had been very human, albeit that one might think of her as a poet's song. As that which inspires it when it is a song such as Dante sang to his Beatrice.

When he returned to the ball-room his father beckoned to him. "What hath become of the de Lessels wench?" he asked. "Hath the abbess whisked her home again to her cloister? Tomorrow I will have the why and wherefore of this mountebanking from her own lips."

"The cloister may not be to the liking of Dame Petronilla," his son suggested. "She did lead me to discover that whiles that we spoke together."

"How so?" his father asked.

"Because I did ask her to wed me, and she did not seem indisposed."

Sir Robert Luffkyn surveyed his son, with many things which unfortunately did not prove unutterable written on his face. When his fury had cooled down into contempt he observed.

"She did not appear indisposed. I trow not. What madness is this that thou hast found in thy cups?"

Humphrey was too taken aback to frame a response. What objection could his father have to a union between a Luffkyn and a de Lessels? It appeared to him most suitable. He ventured to suggest this, when his father had exhausted his comments.

"Surely such a marriage," he said, "would serve to knit our own name with the great tradition of Weepingwold."

His speech could not have been worded more unhappily.

"Yea, and set de Lessels where he was before. Thou wouldst lend thyself to raise a brood of de Lessels that would scorn thy name and thee."

Sir Robert pulled himself together.

"The cloister will be to the liking of Dame Petronilla for the future," he said, grimly. "She hath a beggar's choice before her. I will have an end to this fooling. Tomorrow I shall learn who hath conspired in this unskilful mumming."

Meanwhile the disappearance of Dame Petronilla had been complete. As complete as that of Cinderella herself. The women guests had not so much as set eyes on the one who had come to rival the charms of the fairest of them. The episode at the end of the banquet was still accepted by the others as a piece of mumming which had been interrupted by Jack the fool before the point had made itself plain. Whoever had been accessory to Petronilla's appearance had escaped identification. When the last guest had departed a single white donkey remained in place of the rows of horses and mules. What had become of Petronilla? On whose pillion had she ridden away from the feast?

.  .  .  .  .

As may be imagined, the disappearance of Petronilla from Gracerood on the day upon which the banquet was to take place at Luffkynwold had caused the Abbess the gravest anxiety.

She was not without a clue as to Petronilla's probable destination. Her wild pupil had mounted Neddy—Neddy was likewise missing—and headed for the scene of the festivities. It would be quite like Petronilla. Had she not run away back to Weepingwold once before, on the occasion when the good little parson had returned her safe and sound? The question was whether to pursue her or to await her return when she had realised the madness of the escapade.

When the hours passed and there was no Petronilla the Abbess sent out a search party to scour the wold. If the crazy child had reached Luffkynwold she would be safe enough, at any rate. If not——?

The search party returned without news of the truant.

When, next morning, the great Sir Robert Luffkyn himself, accompanied by his son and Sir Christopher the parson, were seen approaching, the Abbess breathed a sigh of thanksgiving. It meant that Petronilla was safe.

Sir Robert Luffkyn had brought his son and the parson to witness the coming interview. When the Abbess presented herself in the guest's parlour, he came to the point with his usual precision.

By what right had the Abbess of Gracerood permitted his ward, Petronilla de Lessels, to attend the festivities at Luffkynwold on the previous day?

"Then she is safe," the Abbess cried. "God be thanked."

"If she is safe she is safe with you," Sir Robert said. "She left the castle last night."

The other gazed at him, aghast. Last night? Then where was Petronilla now?

"Doubtless with the persons who supplied her with her finery," Luffkyn said. "She was arrayed like Solomon in all his glory."

It was evident that the Abbess was no accessory in the matter. She was gazing at him incredulous of the words she was hearing.

Hilda de Hinton was feeling the groundwork of her faith in human nature giving way under her feet. She could believe anything in the nature of an impulsive escapade of Petronilla. But duplicity, scheming, untruth. Better that they had brought news of her death by misadventure than this.

Sir Robert was right, there must be accomplices. But who could they be?

Sir Robert shrugged his shoulders. Surely the lady whom he was speaking to should know that better than he? He had placed the girl in her charge. There was a cock and bull story of a beggar at the gate. She had been last seen hunting for the aforesaid beggar. "The sooner she takes the vows that bind her to the cloister, the better," he ended.

But Hilda de Hinton shook her head. "Petronilla has proved that she has no call to the cloister," she said. "If I receive her back it will be simply as one living in my charge."

Luffkyn stared at her. He remembered that he had come up against this little, pale woman before.

"We have first to find her," he observed, grimly. "Then—there are plenty of convents willing enough to take her on my terms."

He waited, noting the effect of his words.

"You will have the charity to let me have tidings of her when she is found," the Abbess said. That was all. Her voice was faint and there were tears in her eyes.

The other raised his eyebrows. He had found a lever to use with this good lady whose views he greatly longed to bring into line with his own. "Why so?" he queried. "Your interest in Dame Petronilla appears to have ceased. If you would fain learn of her whereabouts when they come to light, it is still in your power to do so."

The other remained silent. Humphrey who, with Sir Christopher, had remained a silent witness of the duel, felt a sudden access of interest in the Abbess Hilda. She had winced under the words.

He was wincing, too, with the agony of it all. Where was Petronilla?

But she retained the mastery, this little, slightly-built woman. "I am greatly to blame," she said, "that a stricter watch and ward were not kept over the child. It is but just that I should be deprived of her custody. I was to blame, too, that I did not make her understand her true position."

"That in sooth, may be counted blameworthy," Luffkyn said.

He had scored, for the Abbess was frankly ashamed.

"I did not wish her to choose between religion and beggary," she murmured. "The substance of all giving, be it to God, is in the intention. She believed that she had great possessions and it would have counted as such."

With an inexplicable feeling of intense satisfaction, the man of princely benefactions suddenly felt himself towering over the implacable little lady. His concrete mind saw nothing but childish sentimentality in the words. The Abbess was but a foolish woman with a foolish woman's fancies. How could anyone renounce a thing which did not belong to them? The nun was every bit as bad as the child.

"Pooh!"

The interview ended on a note of scorn rather than anger. But Gracerood was plainly no place for Petronilla for more reasons than one. When the girl's whereabouts were discovered Sir Robert would see to it that she was placed somewhere where his infatuated son would not be able to find her. Gracerood would, in any case, be unsafe on that count.

# Chapter XV

*God's Cinderella*

SIR ROBERT and his son had taken their departure, and the Abbess and Sir Christopher were left together. The latter had lingered on because he wished to say something. He had to put a plea in for Petronilla. He had pleaded her cause once before. There was something that appealed to him in Petronilla. It was full seven years since the episode of the mystery play and she was still a child. Little Brother Kit, who had withstood the maturing influences of a parochial charge could not but feel in touch with the spirit which placed Petronilla at a disadvantage with the grown-up world. Even if Jonah had fallen foul of the whale he had set out to swallow, still it was an immense little lady who had set about the task.

"Good mother," he ventured, hesitatingly, "thou wilt surely not refuse to take the little dame back, so doth she return to thee?"

But Hilda de Hinton was not to be moved. Petronilla's heroics were well enough for play-acting. In real life she must play the part which she was prepared to sustain. It was harshly said, but the abbess's heart was in torment. Petronilla had deceived her. There was more behind this escapade. Where was she now? And with whom?

Christopher ventured again. "But it was soothly her intention to return to religion." She would surely be returning and the mother would not refuse her?

The Abbess drew in her lips. "It would take a more severe novitiate than I could give," she said, "to test Petronilla's stability."

Then she glanced more gently at the little shepherd. "Petronilla still hath a champion in thee," she said. "Poor child, that which she dreameth is ever real to her. She lives in her dreams and maketh the dreaming the doing."

"Yet in pursuing her dream she seemeth to be uncommon alert in the doing," was the somewhat unlooked-for rejoinder.

"That is true," the Abbess admitted. There was certainly an alarmingly practical side to Petronilla. "She is a strange child. But she must serve her novitiate elsewhere than here if she wishes to enter religion."

"Did she serve it faithfully elsewhere thou wouldst not then refuse her?"

Christopher asked the question wistfully. He had made himself Petronilla's champion by virtue of a common weakness for dreaming realities, and regarding cold facts as passing shadows. Was it possible that the phantom called the World could have consolidated for Petronilla's vision? The world was very wicked, and its Prince very cunning. Poor little Petronilla!

The Abbess was regarding him, as he stood there pondering, with her mother's eye. He, too, was very young. The Prior of Bycross had called him an angel. At Weepingwold they called him a saint. Poor Christopher! And they had dragged him to the ford to play the part of the ferryman and to carry—the Christ.

He was waiting wistfully for her answer. "Thou wouldst not then refuse her?" he repeated.

"Surely not," she said.

.         .         .         .         .

Humphrey Luffkyn rode away from Gracerood with his father.

The two maintained a somewhat embarrassing silence. Humphrey was relieved when a broken saddle strap compelled him to dismount and attend to the injury. Sir Robert rode on and he was left to himself, sitting by the roadside.

A couple of yokels came walking past. The disgustingness of it! They were discussing Petronilla's appearance at the feast. The gossip had already got abroad. One of the pair shook his head, knowingly. "I do say it be the doing of the witch. They say that she hath been seen about the place. Some do say that she was at the banquet herself."

They caught sight of the master's son and tugged their forelocks and passed on at an accelerated pace.

Humphrey glowered after them. What tongues these people had!

Then he caught sight of Sir Christopher approaching. The latter dismounted when he saw Humphrey and offered his services. He had some cunning as a saddler.

"I have need of one that hath some cunning at prayer," the other told him. "I have inherited some tricks in the matter of treating leather, but I would fain learn the way to conjure Heaven to find the Lady Petronilla for me."

There was something in his companion that invited confidence. He found himself telling the priest the whole story of how Petronilla had been in his company; and how she had suddenly remembered the beggar and had thought that she had seen him, and had run off and never returned.

Sir Christopher sat thinking for a long time.

"Tell me," he said, at length. "Did thou also see this poor beggar?"

"Nay," Humphrey said, "but she described him to me."

"In what wise?"

Humphrey reflected. "She said he was hungry and ill. She would not have it that he was ugly." He paused.

Sir Christopher—or was it little Brother Kit? whose eye was ever on the Unseen?—was thinking. When he had sorted out his ideas he put the question very simply.

"Did she say he had a face like Jesu Christ?" he asked.

Humphrey sent a startled glance in his direction.

"She said he was—beautiful. Yea, as beautiful as Christ on the cross."

Christopher nodded his head. His face had lighted up and become radiant—even as it might have done had he suddenly sighted the lost Petronilla in the distance.

"Then all is well," he said. "Our Lord and all His blessed saints be with her! Wherever she be no harm will touch her." Then he added, softly. "'Tis the clean of heart that see God."

Humphrey watched his face. "Tell me where she is now," he conjured him. This man was seeing things!

But the other shook his head. "Wherever it be that she wanders," he said, "and the world is very wicked, there will be One with her that hath His hand on her shoulder, and no evil thing shall come up to her. All shall be well."

Then he murmured under his breath. "Poor little Petronilla!"

Humphrey sprang up. He faced him. "Tell me more," he cried.

The other opened his eyes in surprise. "But I can tell thee no more," he said, gently. "I know not more than this, that all shall be well with her, and we shall see that all be well—either here or hereafter."

"But I want to see it now!" was the anguished retort. Humphrey was of the earth earthy, and he was in a hurry.

But the man with his eyes on the hills was no necromancer. He practised but the cold, white magic of the chaste Lady, St. Faith. "We must wait on God's time," he said, "and trust. Charity indeed, be greater than faith and hope, but of faith and hope be born the charity that seeketh not her own."

Humphrey was at a loss whether to be impatient or not. He was intrigued by this unlettered man's wisdom. He was used to those who quoted wisdom from books, but not to one who appeared to be reading his on the skyline.

It was a hard saying, this wisdom. It laid a lash about the curiosity which the soothsayer is out to allay.

The clowns had said that the witch was back. *She* might be willing to find Petronilla for him? He thought this defiantly. Then he recoiled from the idea. Petronilla would worship this strong, chaste mystery—the faith which has no truck with the senses. He must not lose Petronilla twice over.

They sat for some time in companionable silence. Then they rose to their feet. There was a sound near-by as of someone approaching.

"Think you," Humphrey said, "that my father will in sooth send Petronilla to some place of his choosing if he finds her?"

"I fear me that will be so," Christopher answered. "I did just now plead my best with the Mother Abbess to take her back, but she hath made up her mind."

"Thou art sure?"

"Soothly."

Christopher looked over his shoulder, hesitatingly as they rode onward. "I thought I did hear a cry as of a poor beast in pain," he said. "I do hope that it were not some poor creature caught in a snare."

.        .        .        .        .

But it was no snared animal which had uttered the cry.

Petronilla de Lessels had passed the night in the hermit's cell. She had made her way there blindly after a futile search for the beggar. She must change back into her own clothes and return home. There could be no returning to the ball, even if she had wished, for her thin shoes were torn to shreds with walking over the rough ground. But she had no wish to return. All her thoughts were with the beggar. He was probably lying dead from hunger somewhere on the wold. All because she had been too proud to carry the food to him herself. Had not Mother Abbess always told her that pride was her besetting sin?

It was terrifyingly dark on the wold. When she had reached the cell in the hollow she had been thankful to crouch down and stay there for the night, once more garbed in her own clothes. She fell asleep and dreamt of Humphrey Luffkyn's new world and of a world that she was guarding with a sword of flame. A world full of noble and curious things. Things of beauty, the love-songs of poets.

Next morning she woke up exceedingly hungry, and the hunger reminded her of the beggar. She must hasten back to Gracerood—on foot, for she had left Neddy behind, but that would be a fitting penance. It was good to be hungry, too, for the beggar had been hungry. Now she understood what it felt like. It was good to be hungry, but—it hurt! It hurt twice over: once for its own pain, and again for the pain of thinking of the other's.

She would be getting her meal soon, but he—he might be lying dead. She pondered the thought until an idea struck her. She would not return to Gracerood until she was much, much hungrier. She would stay out on the wold and do her penance, then she would return to Gracerood and beg the Mother to let her dwell in a cell solitary and so expiate her sin. Yes, she would trudge back to Gracerood and be a beggar for love of the Kingdom of Heaven. And soothly Sister Alys would not have to tell her the story of Cinderella for she had been Cinderella herself!

.    .    .    .    .

It was a long trudge to Gracerood. Petronilla was faint with fatigue and hunger when the last mile was reached. She turned off the road into the undergrowth where she might sit down and rest. How thankful she would be to be home again. The Mother would probably be vexed with her. She must have wondered what had become of her.

Suddenly she pulled up. There was a sound of voices, men's voices. Here on the lonely wold. Then she saw two horses without their riders. She caught sight of the latter. They were seated on the roadside with their backs turned to her. A sudden thrill went through her. One of them was her companion of last night. And the other? The other was Sir Christopher the priest. Humphrey was saying something. She could not help catching the words:

"Think you that my father will in sooth send Petronilla to some place of his choosing if he finds her?"

Then came the answer.

"I fear me that will be so. I did just now plead my best with the Mother Abbess to take her back but she hath made up her mind."

"Art thou sure?" came the question.

And the answer:

"Soothly."

.        .        .        .        .

They had mounted their horses and ridden on. Petronilla was standing, rigid, staring in front of her.

Mother Abbess was not going to take her back. She sat herself down and slowly thought it out. If she went to Mother Abbess she would not indeed turn her out, but she would hand her over to Robert Luffkyn to put her in some place of his choosing. The Law regarded Robert Luffkyn in some way as her guardian. She had grasped that much. Guardians had great power over their wards. The Crown might abet Robert Luffkyn in his choice?

There was Robert Luffkyn's son, and his world. She had taken a sip of the cup which she was to renounce. The Mother Abbess would send her back to that world—to the poet with the reverent eyes that had looked into hers. . . .

She took a long look at the patch on the horizon which was Gracerood. She was very, very hungry, and tired and cold. As hungry and tired and cold as the beggar himself. . . . What had become of the beggar?

She rose to her feet and walked mechanically, in the direction that led away from Gracerood. There was the shelter of the hermit's cell, if she had the strength to walk back.

On the road she met a woman with a little child. The woman gave a sharp glance at her. Petronilla had not the courage to ask her for a bite of bread. She had yet to learn to be a real beggar.

Later on, when she was getting near to Weepingwold, she met another woman, who gave her a slice of bread and some apples. To these the good soul added a word of warning.

"If thou be seeking alms," she said, "go not near to the cottage in yon hollow. 'Tis the house of a witch. She left it empty for many years, but she hath been seen about the place, and by now she is doubtless back there practising her devilry."

The witch! A sick horror seized hold of Petronilla. A witch had lived in the hermit's cell. It was a witch's garb which she had borrowed. And only the mercy of Heaven had saved her from actual contact with the evil occupant. But for this warning she might have walked into her refuge and found it in possession of its sinister tenant.

But what was she to do? Her place of refuge was gone. Not for worlds would she risk an encounter with the witch. Better far die here out on the wold. Another night was approaching. She sat down once more by the roadside, homeless. The woman with the child whom she had met a while since was returning that way. The child was running behind his mother. He paused as he passed her. Petronilla leant forward and offered him an apple. He put out a hand to take it, then darted away, terrified, at a sharp call from his mother. The little rebuff brought the sense of desolation in her heart to an unbearable point. She was homeless and friendless—a very perfect Cinderella.

She crept on as far as the cross tracks, they could not be called roads. The people of Luffkynwold had erected a wayside cross at the meeting of the ways. Petronilla crept up to it. She looked up at the face of the Figure on the cross.—The eyes! There was something familiar about the eyes!

There was a clatter of horses' feet. Petronilla glanced along the road. Without doubt it was a search party. They were seeking for her. They would carry her back to comfort, food and warmth, and—human affection. A vision of her companion of—was it only last night?—rose before her eyes. The story of Cinderella has for one of its characters a prince.

The Christ on the cross looked down and watched.

She had no means of escaping them. So she remained sitting where she was.

They were close on her now, and one of them was saying something to his companion. She had been recognised.

Dame Petronilla de Lessels had come to the end of her escapade. The riders were passing the wayside cross and the Christ stretched upon it was watching Petronilla.

# Chapter XVI

## *Re-enter Astrotha*

T WAS THE SUNDAY morning after the house-warming and the parson was engaged in framing his discourse to be delivered at mid-day Mass. The disturbing events of the last two days had put him in arrears with it. Now, to add to his troubles, it had been intimated that Sir Robert Luffkyn and his guests were intending to assist at the parochial Mass. Sir Amyas, the chaplain with an Oxford background and a Parisian halo, would be assisting as well, and Christopher was on his beam ends. A little method in the making of his sermon might have made amends for a restricted vocabulary, but the parson's was a method only suited to the flock who listened to them. The frightened sheep were marvellously at home in church in these days. He had a way of illustrating his point with a story. There would be subtlety in the point but great simplicity in the story. Little Brother Kit read stories into every occurrence in life, and everything that came under his eye. Sometimes he told the story to God—it had been his uncouth effort at mental prayer when Brother Paul had tried to teach him to be methodical in his prayer. Other times, God seemed to be telling the story to him. Now-a-days the stories came to his aid when he was expected to preach discourses without any learning at his disposal. After all, the Master had spoken in parables, and the Kingdom of Heaven was like unto so many queer little things that happened. It spoke loudly and insistently in the things of everyday life.

Christopher knew perfectly well what he wanted to say on this occasion. He wanted to warn his flock against the inordinate desire of the right hand to let the left hand know what it was doing. Christopher's sermons were always, so to speak, preached from the Mount. The good people of his parish were not slow at giving, indeed they were almost lavish, some of them, but one and all, they dearly loved receiving the praise of men for their actions. It troubled their pastor not a little. It seemed to him that Satan stepped in and gobbled up what was intended for the delectation of their Heavenly Father. Some holy writer had expressed the idea in language fit for the ears of the gentry, but Christopher had not got the book containing the quotation. He formed a picture in his mind of a bloated and wide-jawed creature of the reptile tribe, waiting to pounce upon and intercept the food offered to One Who, though the Maker of all things, yet condescended to be hungry.

It was almost impossible to apply his mind to his task. Supplied with a steed, his thoughts rode away on the consideration of hunger and intercepted largesse to the story that Humphrey Luffkyn had told him. Where was Petronilla? Was she simply playing Eve on the stage of life? Was she making the incredible mistake of thinking the part of the devil to be a lordly one? These new scholars laughed at those who said the devil had a tail, but, soothly, a tail did serve to remind one that the fiend was no party worthy of respect.

Christopher returned to his sermon with a jerk. What a feather brain he had! He fixed his mental eye rigidly on the dragon with the bulging sides and open mouth.

The door opened and Mrs. Agnes thrust her head in. She made a flimsy excuse for fetching something. I believe it was the leather bottel.

"They do tell me," she observed when she was safely in the room, "that the witch hath returned. Tom Littlework hath seen her and he saith——"

Christopher cast an appealing glance at her. "Tell me of the witch at another time," he said, "I have now my sermon to make." He had already heard this rumour of the reappearance of the witch. It was thrillingly interesting, but there was a time for everything.

"It were well to preach a sermon on witchcraft and the wiles of the devil," Mrs. Agnes opined. "They say Astrotha hath sold herself body and soul to the devil and he hath her in his clutches more than ever."

"By what authority do they say that?" the pastor asked, sharply. He never let pass the idle word that might be a grievous slander.

Mrs. Agnes produced her evidence in somewhat aggrieved self-defence. She had the consolation that it was unanswerable. "She hath no longer the pock-marks on her face," she said, "and there never was a human leech that could take away pock-marks."

Christopher found it safer to remove himself to the church.

So Astrotha was back. He had prayed for her conversion for six years. He had hoped that she might have repented. Ever since that night before her departure when he had caught a glimpse of a figure peeping in the leper's window, and afterwards discovered the black cat with a bit missing from his left ear, in the church, he had cherished hopes for Astrotha, and he had prayed for her—up in the place where Death lay dead—where he built up his rampart round the best things of the better world. On the merry spot that he called "Laughingwold."

.        .        .        .        .

There was still the sermon to make!

He went over in desperation and knelt before the image of the Blessed Mother *Sedes Sapientiæ*. Holy Wisdom was seated on her arm. He was wearing a little white woven shirt that clung tightly to his limbs. It had been washed many times and was now a terribly tight fit. He fetched back his thoughts to his sermon.

Ten minutes later he was striking his breast. Instead of praying for light, or framing the sentences which would not shock the refined ears of his hearers he had been telling himself a story! That came of seeking inspiration from *Sedes Sapientiæ*. But, if it had not been for the presence of Master Reginaldus Catus and other of his ilk who would be present, the story would have come in excellently. It was there, on the tip of his tongue.

In spite of strenuous efforts to the contrary, the thing on the tip of Christopher's tongue remained there. He faced his congregation, when the moment arrived, and, ascending as was his wont, the mount of the beatitudes, gave out his text:

"Let not thy right hand know what thy left hand doeth."

Humphrey Luffkyn, seated next to his friend Catus, was letting his thoughts run on the one absorbing topic. He was asking himself the one, unvarying question: Where was Petronilla? All yesterday he and his trusty friend Catus, had scoured the wold in the forlorn hope of getting a clue. It seemed too certain that the unknown accomplice who had brought her had carried her away. There were terrible possibilities of which Humphrey did not care to think. Petronilla should remain for him a priceless memory. An inspiration. Aye, a Beatrice to make of him a second Dante. But he would not leave a stone unturned until he had satisfied himself of her whereabouts.

Catus was not trying to listen to the sermon either, or rather, he was trying not to listen, but it is hard not to when the sermon is bad enough. The clumsy sentences got on his nerves. The preacher was telling a story. The words came stumbling out.

"Once upon a time, dear children, there was a good wife that did think to fashion a little woven vest for the image of the Christ-Child. 'Twas of wool, and finely woven, and the good wife had great pride in it when it was finished. And so great was her pride that she must needs run hither and thither, crying to her neighbours: 'See you here what a fine vest I have woven with my own hands for the Baby Jesu!' Nor would she be content but that each good wife had the fingering of it until it were so much soiled with the fingering that the good wife aforesaid had need to wash it before she placed it on the image of the Holy Child. And in sooth, in the wash, not only was the wool impoverished so that it was no longer soft and warm, but it also shrank, so that it fitted painful close and clinging to the Babe's body, to His great miscomfort.

"So did the Holy Child Jesu say to Mary His Mother: 'My Mother, see. They did ever bring Me the broken toys that other boys have first played with; and now they bring Me this vest that hath been so much soiled with fingers that it hath been put through the wash, and it hath shrunk so that it sore dis-easeth Me. Fain would I have a little shift made all for Mine own Self; and toys that no other boys have played with first.'"

The preacher cast anxious eyes about for those that had ears to hear. He saw the gaping mouths of the simpletons. He saw also the mouth of Sir Robert Luffkyn gaping, but not from a like cause. The latter's elaborate yawn was the result of vastly diverse reasons.

The Founder of Luffkynwold was making mental notes. This was the flighty youth who held the church ales at the *Travellers' Rest* and gave hospitality to the witch's cat, and whom he had seen, years ago, at a function at Gracerood making grimaces. The Prior's "semi-angel" appeared to have a not too dignified other half! This stuff appeared to go down all right with the yokels.

Then Christopher shot a glance sideways. There was a shadow at the leper's window. It was the window he had once seen the witch peeping through. Could it be Astrotha, repentant, after all? He would have been content to wait for another six years. What would she be thinking of his sermon?

He remained to pray, as was his custom, after Mass was over.

When he came down the church from the sanctuary there was someone kneeling praying before *Sedes Sapientiæ*. It must be someone who had taken the sermon to heart. A sermon preached under such dire circumstances might perhaps hope to produce fruit?

It was a woman. He went up to her and touched her on the shoulder. The face that looked at him was familiar—vaguely so. His heart beat quicker. An Astrotha who had turned from her evil ways. An Astrotha who had lost her hardness might look like this.

He hesitated whether to recognise her or not.

"Child," he said, at length, "didst thou wish to speak with me?"

"Yea, holy father."

"Hast thou made thy confession, child?" he asked.

"Yea, father, a week since."

Then the witch's repentance was an accomplished fact! It had not been his sermon. As usual he had been vain-glorious.

"That is well," he said. "The past can bury its dead. Hast thou anything to trouble thee since?"

She followed him to the simple confessional. At the end of the short recital, when she had received his blessing she glanced up and looked him questioningly in the face.

"Father, dost thou know me?" she asked.

"Soothly," he said. "Thou art Astrotha the witch."

"Astrotha, if you will," came the answer, "but no witch."

She was turning to go when she heard him calling her back.

"I had forgotten to give thee a penance," he reminded her. "For these slight faults, I bid thee do this penance. There is a loom in thy cottage, if I remember rightly. I would have thee weave a little silken shirt of the skeins that I will give thee for the image of the Christ-Child before which I did see thee kneeling just now.

"And now, do thou make a good act of contrition for the sins of thy past life."

.        .        .        .        .

The reappearance of Astrotha the witch had served opportunely as a red herring to divert the village gossip from the unseemly episode of Petronilla's escapade, but in the household of Robert Luffkyn the subject remained very much to the fore. The latter was anxious to transfer his establishment back to the Thames-side manor, for the time being, for his son Humphrey was behaving in a most unconscionable manner.

Humphrey firmly refused to accept the solution to the mystery which was the obvious one. Petronilla would be at present in the keeping of whoever had provided her with her outfit and conveyed her to the castle, but Humphrey refused to believe that the wicked world had claimed her for its own. He had sampled Petronilla's soul. True, she had not told how she had come, or with whom, but he could believe no evil of her. Some fate must have overtaken her out on the wold. Like one demented he rode about, scouring the country round, accompanied by friend Catus, who, under the influence of the charm of Mistress Joan, had a very kind sympathy with his friend.

In the end he presented himself to his father and announced his intention of remaining in Luffkynwold until his search had produced some result.

Sir Robert surveyed his son, grimly. "And what would you do with the baggage if you found her?" he asked.

"I would marry her," Humphrey said, "unless indeed, she did wish to follow the religious life."

Sir Robert surveyed him amusedly. "It doth not occur to you that she is now following the religious life?"

His son stared at him. "You have not found her and placed her in some nunnery other than Gracerood?" he cried.

Luffkyn smiled. "Is it the first time that has occurred to you?" he asked, drily.

"But you would have surely told me." Humphrey was gazing at his father's sphinx-like countenance.

"So that you might go and sing a love-song under her window," the latter said. "But there hath been enough of this foolery. Go and tell the little woman at Gracerood that you have been following a wild goose chase."

So it came to pass that Humphrey Luffkyn returned to his own world, carrying with him the image of an undamaged Petronilla in his heart. Henceforward, he would not lack for inspiration. Petronilla was a window through which he had looked upon a larger world. She and the little parson whom Catus had made the object of his unconscionable jest were of another world than this. Newer than the world that the Spaniard had visioned, and older than the ancient one that was yielding treasures to the poets.

# Chapter XVII

*Roger Beakwhistle Makes Notes*

THERE WAS NO question of it being an idle rumour. Astrotha was occupying her former residence in the hollow. That she had been trafficking with the devil was manifest from the sinister fact that instead of growing older in the intervening years she appeared to have renewed her youth. It was a gentle, almost childlike face that people caught sight of, barely visible through the heavy penitent's veil worn by the ex-witch.

For Astrotha had returned a penitent. She no longer practised her black arts. The gossips shook their heads. It was clear that the devil had done what he so often did, turned on his own and robbed her of her cunning. She eked out a precarious livelihood by spinning the rough homespun cloth favoured by the peasantry. If it had not been for the parson, things would have gone badly with Astrotha, but Sir Christopher saw to it that starvation was kept from the door of the ex-witch. Sometimes when work was direfully slack the occupant of the hermit's cell would creep out and sit with upturned palms by the wayside to wait on the charity of the passer-by. But it was grudging charity, for a witch who has had her claws drawn fares hardly at the hands of the virtuous.

As time went on, indeed, there rose a section of the village, headed by Roger the farmer, who began to say very definite things about the converted Astrotha. Why, they asked, if the witch were truly penitent, had she not done open penance in a sheet in the church? The parson had let her off with reprehensible lightness.

True, she did not intrude herself in church with the others but continued to hear her Mass through the leper's window, but, then that might be part of her pose as a "holy" recluse. The parson would be building her an anchorhold there next! It was known that many a time broken meat from the rectory table had gone to the ex-witch. Bread and water was the right diet for a witch, be she ever so converted.

Gradually, under the auspices of Roger Beakwhistle, it began to be whispered that Astrotha still retained possession of her mysterious powers, and that she had succeeded in bewitching the parson himself. Beneath this pose of a penitent, so it was darkly hinted, Astrotha practised her black arts. It was an "uncanny" success that attended the parson's efforts. All the world was running after him, and he but an unlearned peasant. Why should half a dozen stalwart masons, employed all day in garnishing Luffkynwold Hall with pinnacles, in the style of the king's new palace at Shene, occupy their meagre spare time in erecting a steeple on the church tower simply because the parson had a fancy for a finger longer than his own pointing heavenward? Why, I ask, or, rather, Roger did, should the people crowd the village church like the silly sheep they had turned out (it still rankled!) to hear such sermons as the parson preached, with never a long word in them that a man could not understand? Most sinister of all, the parson had cured a sick cow, Betsy Allen's one and only head of cattle, which had fallen sick of a complaint which Roger with his knowledge knew to be fatal. Of course, the parson attributed it to the intercession of a very efficacious saint, but Roger knew better. He set himself to watch. He knew what to expect of one who had taken on a witch's familiar spirit under the pseudonym of Tibby. Very soon there was a new scandal. Sir Christopher had been seen going into the witch's house, she having sent word that she was dying. And next day she was as well as any! The foolish villagers would have it that the parson had worked a miracle on her behalf. To do the parson justice he had looked uncommon confused when Roger questioned him on the matter—quite frightened, in fact. He had muttered something to the effect that it had been the doing of a saint. What saint? Roger asked, hoping to catch him out by taking him unawares, and he had answered "St. Valarius." Roger had had his misgivings, and on consulting the calendar they had been confirmed. No such saint existed!

Meanwhile, the parish had gone on flourishing like the green bay tree. The parson, in spite of his uncouth speech and ways— he had his opposite in Sir Amyas, Sir Robert Luffkyn's chaplain, who could hold his own with any knight in the shire—could turn people round with his little finger. True, his turning set them with their backs to their sins, but these things can be a blind. The church was resplendent with gifts from the poorest—those that had erstwhile spent their pennies on the witch. St. Mary Magdalen still wore Mrs. Lyons' satin gown, but one might not gainsay the gift for Mrs. Lyons and her lodger had at last been made true man and wife at the church door. Still—it all went but to prove one thing. Roger Beakwhistle had found the solution to the mystery of the parson's phenomenal influence.

Much of the evidence was damning in itself. Two or three times a week Sir Christopher might be seen slipping off to the wold, and it had been discovered that his objective was the tomb! Who could make a trysting-place of so sinister a spot but one who was out to meet a witch, and that to no good end? Then there was always Tom's story of the parson's bottle with the love potion in it. And to conclude, quite a number of people had heard Sir Christopher speak of "St. Valarius" in connection with things that needed explaining.

The leaven of malice and wickedness thus set in action was not slow in taking effect. Christopher became conscious that something was wrong. He felt the changed atmosphere. The well-behaved people who patronised the *Luffkyn Arms* were adopting a suspicious attitude towards the parson. The latter naturally set down the fault to himself. The people who looked askance at him were law-abiding folk. Christopher felt the sins of his beloved black sheep heavy on his shoulders. It was surely a direct visitation from Heaven, this discovery of his real worth, because he had become vain-glorious over his church, and the resurrection of the dead village. And yet he had been truly terrified at the praise of men. Well, thanks be to God, he was now to be protected from it. Nevertheless, it was hard to bear, this covert antagonism and reproach. Christopher often looked at his anointed hands in these days before he said Mass and wondered if they were truly soiled in the sight of God and His angels. If so, he had but soiled them in the calling of others to salvation. God would have mercy on his soul.

There was another who came in for a hard time in these days. It was the inmate of the hermit's cell. It is safe and easy to throw mud—real mud—at a witch who has ceased to practise her arts. There was a third section in the village who without regarding the parson as a saint, or on the other hand, blackening him with Roger's brush, yet held that the little pastor had been in some way injured by the witch. It was an easier way of showing good-will to the parson than leading a decent life, to insult the woman who was supposed to be the secret enemy of his soul. Astrotha never practised her arts on any save the parson. It was barely safe now-a-days for the occupant of the cell in the hollow to walk abroad. Baiting the witch became quite a favourite pastime. Nobody's cow fell sick in consequence, nor was the assailant attacked by a wasting disease. All this went on unknown to Sir Christopher or it would have been stopped at once. Even bull-baiting and cock-fighting were abhorrent in his eyes. The witch apparently never told him of the treatment to which she was subjected.

It was just upon a year since the family had been in residence. The new house which had been duly warmed by the banquet which had been the scene of Petronilla de Lessels' short appearance in public had had time to cool again when it was notified that Sir Robert Luffkyn and his retinue were returning to the hall. Dame Isabella had agreed to hold her nose and undergo a short visit there. The attractions of her other home had increased with the wealth and social importance of her husband, and Sir Robert the tanner had become monstrously rich. So rich, in fact, that danger lay in the accumulation of further wealth. The king's tax-gatherers had become excessively interested in Robert Luffkyn's "treasure of gold." His Majesty the King was watching Luffkynwold and its many chimneys as a dog watches the cat eat its dinner. There is small satisfaction in accumulating wealth the bulk of which goes out in taxes; moreover, the bulk itself may become a dangerous bait where avarice is the dominant vice of the reigning monarch. In many ways Luffkynwold had been a disappointment.

Dame Isabella Luffkyn still protested against a prolonged residence on the ancestral soil even as had done her ancestor by marriage Robin the serf. Humphrey became every day more a man of letters, and deeply attached to the haunts of learning. People wondered that he did not enter one of the great monasteries, but he remained a scholar out in the world. He had announced his intention to his father of remaining single until he was satisfied that Dame Petronilla de Lessels was finally bound by the ties of religion. Luffkyn was not unduly disturbed. Humphrey was developing on clerkish lines. A visionary lady-love might keep him from rushing off into a monastery and becoming a monk. A vision was far more likely to hold his freakish offspring in thrall than flesh and blood. In time the right flesh and blood would come along. The pursuit of scholarship had not prevented Humphrey's friend Catus from following the ways of ordinary humanity. His devotion to Joan Luffkyn was obvious, and not disapproved of by her father. Catus had an European fame and it was no light honour, and an additional triumph for the house of Luffkyn. The union, moreover, would work in all right with the Bycross branch of the business. Luffkyn and Catus were really out for the same end—the making of books.

But all this time things had not been going well with Master Catus. He carried his left arm in a sling and made curt replies to those who enquired as to his ailment. Humphrey wondered what was wrong with his friend. He no longer paid visits to their house and his sister Joan had become very much a maiden all forlorn.

Catus had grown to be more than ever out against the established order of things. Men, to excuse their lack of learning, cried out that the gate of Heaven was low and men must stoop to enter it. These men accepted everything that the Church taught in the same way that he, Catus, accepted the incomprehensible doctrine of the Blessed Trinity. Catus, in fact, had turned his attention from the wort on the nose to the feature itself. And his laughter had already provoked many to mock at that of which the nose itself was a feature. Master Catus, in short, carried his soul as well as his arm in a sling. On more counts than one he was in a pretty bad way.

·        ·        ·        ·        ·

John Appleyard had got his report ready for his master. It was an eminently satisfactory one. Pretty well everything pestiferous had been eliminated from Luffkynwold. Milk and honey had been more or less accepted as the ideal diet at the *Luffkyn Arms*. The church was well attended on Sundays and week-days. When John Appleyard came to this point he hesitated, as he had done before. There was a disquieting fact in connection with this last item. He cleared his throat.

"The people," he said, "are saying that the parson, Sir Christopher Plimsett be bewitched. Astrotha, the woman that lived in the hollow hath returned, and the parson is much in her company."

Robert Luffkyn considered. It sounded foolish enough, but he knew the matchless Mariquita by other fame than that of a witch.

She could certainly turn a shaveling like Christopher Plimsett round on her little finger.

"There be certain other things," John Appleyard went on. "People do say that this Astrotha leads a double life. Here she would pose as a penitent, but she hath been lately seen at Greathampton in other habit. Wat, the man that did bide with Sir Christopher at the rectory at the outset of his ministry, and who did ever have it that he was not the holy man that folks would believe, having had some shewing on the point at the rectory, did recognise Astrotha by the marks on her face."

"There be more than one woman in England marked with small-pox," Luffkyn said. "I call not that evidence."

"Nay," was the response, "but it was held against Astrotha that she should be in two places at once and change her complexion at will, for those that have seen her here noted not the pock marks."

Luffkyn nodded towards the door. "Go now," he said. "But, wait—— Find the one that hath these things to say concerning the parson and send him to me."

A summons to appear before the Lord of the Manor gave Roger Beakwhistle a nasty jar. What (and which?) was it that he was wanted for? It was truly reassuring to find that the great man was merely in search of evidence concerning the parson's conduct.

Roger, his knees no longer shaking, ticked off each indictment on a dirty finger.

The parson had turned his cattle out of their shelter, but that was years ago.

"Fudge! I did that. Get on," Sir Robert said.

The parson had dealings with the witch. Tom Littlework had found his leather bottle outside her house and thrown it at the devil.

"What else?" the other asked.

The witch was mainly fed from the rectory table, and the parson kept tryst with her, since he durst not go and see her in her own house, at the tomb on the wold. Anyone would tell how the parson was constantly seen going there, and what else could his business be?

"Something that is not thy business," Sir Robert retorted. "Get out with you." He pointed to the door, and Roger got out—but not before he had delivered his last word.

"He hath invented a saint that doth not exist, and he calleth him 'Valarius the wonder-worker.'"

Sir Robert sat pulling his beard and thinking. There was a flippant touch about this last indictment. It lent colour to some of the others. There might be something behind it all?

That same afternoon Sir Robert Luffkyn happened to catch sight of Sir Christopher. He was walking rapidly in the direction of the wold. Here was an opportunity of finding out what the young fool did do. He was unmistakably heading for the tomb. It would certainly be an excellent place for a rendezvous.

Luffkyn followed. When the priest reached the tomb, he gave a swift, furtive glance round him, and then disappeared within. It was certainly peculiar conduct. The man of action crept noiselessly up to the entrance and listened. There were no voices so far, only a curious "swish, swish." Then the eavesdropper heard Sir Christopher's voice say something—in rather amused tones.

"Dear Lord, I be taking them for Mrs. Lyons that hath had her penance finished, last week! 'Tis my scatter-brain! But I pray Thee take them as for the sins of Roger Beakwhistle."

Then there was more "swish, swish."

Sir Robert crept away even more silently than he had approached. An hour later he summoned his bailiff. "See that this message be delivered to Roger Beakwhistle," he said, and handed the other a missive.

Roger Beakwhistle, being sufficiently scholared, fortunately read the anonymous message himself. It ran:

"It hath been found out. Fly if thou value thy safety."

Roger's whole person shook like a jelly. If he only knew which the "it" was he might put together a few fictions and prepare a defence, but there were so many possibilities. There was nothing for it but to take the advice given. That same night must find him roofless, as roofless as his evicted cattle, the same that Sir Christopher had turned out when he became a shepherd of souls.

# Chapter XVIII

*"Christopher! Christopher!"*

T HE STEEPLE on Christopher's church had suddenly stopped growing. The building of it had been stopped as it had been judged unsafe to continue it. Owing to the weakness of the tower, there was fear of a collapse. The parson looked on it and read there a glum parable. He was thoroughly sick of everything and the finger which should have pointed Heavenward, albeit with but a stump, had received a twist and Christopher was reading a message after the dickins's own heart. Desolation had gripped his soul and he was yielding to the sin of sadness.

It was one thing to suffer from the malice of an enemy—that he had done gladly—and Luffkynwold had indeed provided its whips of little cords. The cross had to be borne, and persecution and calumny were to be joyfully accepted. (They were unspeakable, the things they said about him.) But was it right that he, little Brother Kit, should be fancying himself the right man in a place of consequence, such as Weepingwold had become? How much better suited to the position he held was Sir Amyas. Sir Amyas had preached for him on the last occasion, and Sir Christopher had only understood about half of what he was saying. Why should his flock be deprived of a pastor possessing such superior qualifications simply because Kit Plimsett had been taken on as a stop-gap, and his patron's good feeling prevented him from sending him back to his right place? No wonder men had come to regard him with black looks, or else looks of pity. The steeple was certainly an emblem of the pastor. What wisdom it would be to take the warning before his growing pride tottered to its final fall and Christopher Plimsett, parson of Luffkynwold, lay a heap of loose stones round about the tower which was Kit the carter's son.

The Prior would surely take him back, and he could begin his novitiate all over again. His beloved Bycross rose before his eyes. He could pray there for his poor black sheep. They would not lose the only thing that he could give them. He could say Mass there as well as here. He thrilled at the thought of saying Mass at Bycross. It was not the Bycross of old days, he knew well, but Heaven was the place for such joys as the old time Bycross had provided. Such things were too good for this world. It would be for the best, and the benefice of Luffkynwold would be vacant for Sir Amyas to dignify it with his learning and other edifying attributes.

Christopher, in short, had made up his mind to do what, some centuries later a parish priest whose sanctity was later confirmed by the Church, likewise attempted—run away!

One morning after Mass, having set his affairs in due order, he knelt before the altar reviewing his past.

The church was wonderfully different from what he had found. It bore evidence on every side of being the community home of the hearts of his people. It was the place where their spiritual being expressed itself in the vernacular. It was a rude and uncouth *patois*, but to Christopher it all appeared very comely. The figure of the Christ-Child, seated on His Mother's arm was clad in a garment of ample dimensions and dazzling whiteness. Whiter than any fuller could have made it—so Christopher told himself. It never appeared to take the dirt like the other draperies. It was thought to be the gift of the Abbess of Gracerood, and Christopher had allowed the impression to remain. It might not be wise to let the people know that it came from the loom in the cottage in the hollow. People were so prejudiced against its inmate. For just a year and a day she had lived her penitential life, and heard her Mass through the squint, like a leper. Things would indeed go hard with her were she to be left without a protector when Luffkynwold knew him no more, but he had arranged otherwise—very much otherwise.

The silver dove was hanging in its place, very bright and shining. It was still his own hand that kept it so. His heart had been single, at any rate. He thought of his first Mass. He hoped his poor sheep would not be shy of Sir Amyas and huddle up in the corner, so to speak, when a scholar in a fur tippet addressed them from the new alabaster pulpit. There might be a new image of Our Lady as well, in alabaster, like the beautiful statues at Bycross, and her Child would stand in no need of a woven shirt. His poor sheep would assuredly huddle against the wall in expectation of Wat, the outside man, and his stick!

Then he thought of the bell-rope and his bruised hands. Since then he had surely been through the dure process—like that of the flail and winepress, which is his part who would make bread and wine into the sacred Body and Blood?

He cast a last upward glance at the pyx.

"Christopher!" he seemed to hear a voice cry. Insistently:

"Christopher! Christopher!"

But, no, it was his imagination. The church was empty save for the Presence of Him that dwelt in the pyx.

.        .        .        .        .

He went back into the house. He had to write a message of farewell to the Abbess of Graceroad. She had been his true friend and advisor for these years. He might indeed have consulted her on this step. And he might have bade her adieu in person? Had Christopher asked himself why he had not done so he might have discerned the spirit that had taken him, so to put it, to the pinnacle of his steeple and preached a plausible parable.

The message would be carried over in the course of the day. It contained more than a mere word of farewell. There was matter of importance in it.

There was one more place that he would like to have visited. It was the place of resurrection on the "laughing" wold. But it might reprove him in his weeping mood. He felt strangely shy of the place where joy had triumphed, sitting on the gate of death and peering into its futile fastness. How often the happy sword of love had pierced him out there where Death lay dead.

No, he would not say good-bye to the laughing wold. It might be laughing at him.

He packed up a few of his possessions. Just the few that he could not leave behind for his successor. He came across one that gave him a sharp twinge of conscience. It was the obit of the Abbot Valarius. He ought to have returned it to Master Catus ages ago. He had kept it more than a year. And it contained the Abbess of Gracerood's contribution to the appreciations of the holy Abbot. The Abbess had written in Greek, so Christopher had not been able to peruse it. He thrust the roll into his wallet. Some day Master Catus might come to Bycross and he would return it to him. Or Master Humphrey Luffkyn would probably be coming that way. The family were already in residence and had he found the obit sooner he could have entrusted it to him. At any rate, he would not leave it behind for Sir Amyas.

He cast a last look back, as he rode away, at the village which had been his cure of souls, with its church with the unfinished steeple, and the tannery with its consummated chimneys. There was a rumour abroad that the king had got his eye on Sir Robert Luffkyn and his enterprises, and that the "Luffkyn Lord" of Weepingwold had need to keep a sharp watch and ward over his "treasure of gold." He wondered if it were true.

It was night time when Floss bore her rider into the meadows round about Bycross Priory. Christopher slipped in quietly. He knew the way to do so. His intention was to catch the Prior as he came down from his cell for night office. He would waylay him in the scriptorium and beg of him re-admission into the order. He would confess his failure and ask pity on his shortcomings.

Bycross seemed amazingly still! The tall grey gables of the dwelling house rose above the cloister. Behind the narrow windows the monks would be sleeping, getting their rest before night office. Was it in comparison with the noise and bustle of his last visit that Bycross seemed so still? It seemed to possess a hush even more tangible than in the old days when he had prayed among the lilies in the Prior's garden. Soon the lights would twinkle in the dormer windows and the brothers would be coming down to the chapel and there would be, in the stillness of the night, life and wakefulness the more intense for the peace lying round.

The beauty and restfulness of it was almost painful in its sweetness. The soft air carried the scent of shy night perfumes. The printing press, with its clatter, seemed like a nightmare, or one of the things which were prayed against at compline. This place, where soon the sound of matins and lauds would be flinging prayer and praise into the light side of the scale weighed down by the wild dongs of the world, wrapped its peace round him like a mantle. It was marvellous. The intervening years seemed to have melted away. This was surely the Bycross of his own day? Of eight years ago. It seemed like twenty!

He made his way to the cloister which formed the scriptorium, or had done so until the advent of the machines had made that a misnomer.

Where were the printing presses? Christopher stood looking round in wonder. They had all disappeared. The space where they had stood was empty. A faint light which had been left burning in a far corner enabled him to remark all this. The place was even as it had been in the old days. The Bycross of his heart's love had been given back to him. He must surely be dreaming?

He found himself wondering who had left the light burning? It was so like one of his old tricks. Old Brother Paul would have to form little Brother Kit all over again. The parson of Luffkynwold had got out of the way of things!

He went over to where the light was burning. A desk stood there. One of the old scriptorium desks. The others had not been replaced. He gave a start. Someone was seated at it. Someone who had been sitting writing and had fallen asleep at his task, for the shaven head was resting on the book.

Christopher crept close up. It was Brother Paul himself. He must have come back after night prayers to finish his task. It was a strange thing for a monk to do. It must be something very urgent for night prayers finished the day's work. He peered over the sleeping man's shoulder at the open page.

It was the last chapter of the Book of the Apocalypse and the pen had fallen from the writer's hand as he finished the last word.

"Surely I come quickly: Amen. Come, Lord Jesus."

Christopher read the words. As he read the last word—it was traced in a shaky hand but perfect in every curve, he drew in his breath.

Joy. Enlightenment. Sweetness. Unction. They had all come to Brother Paul, spelling the letters of that holy Name; flooding his soul, striking one full chord of music. And at the end had come—sleep, for, Christopher remembered, He giveth His beloved sleep.

He glanced down at the head resting there. He was fain to waken Brother Paul for he had discovered that he needed counsel. He needed it badly, and Brother Paul had always been his counsellor.

A voice was crying in his ear: "Christopher!"

"Christopher, Christopher! What hast thou done with the Christ?"

What had he done with the Christ? Back on the wold, in his cure of souls, the "tardiest wight" might be calling for him now.

He had forgotten the "tardiest wight." It was all as clear as clear. He realised it now. He had turned his back on his duty. He must get back as soon as possible, before harm had been done. Brother Paul would surely tell him that.

Should he waken Brother Paul? He debated the point for a moment. No, he would not. Why should he? Surely Brother Paul had counselled him already when he inscribed the holy Name Jesus.

The joy in his heart had been followed by enlightenment. There was sorrow now, for his error; and this adorable Bycross was sending him forth for ever. But with the tearing of his heartstrings, there came unction; and with unction sweetness. And with all, Love, for is it not true that Love be at the core and in the summing.

Christopher stooped and gently touched the thick fringe of white hair. It seemed very chill and draughty round about where Brother Paul was sleeping, but they would find him soon and take him to bed. He must be very, very tired, but he had finished his work.

The lights were already beginning to shine out through the dormer windows when Christopher turned to give his last look at Bycross. The thin train of white-robed monks was making its way to the chapel through the scriptorium. Father Prior walked with bowed head, for two days back the King's officers had arrived and confiscated the press set up by Robert Luffkyn without a royal warrant. Bycross had narrowly escaped suppression.

They were the ancient remnant, for the novices had been removed with the machinery. The Prior caught sight of the light at the end of the scriptorium. Followed by two or three of the brothers he hastened over to find out the cause.

It was poor old Brother Paul. He had carried the M.S., which he hoped to finish before the Lord called him, back to his former quarters where he had worked in the old days with pen and scalpel, and quietly resumed his task. He had leave to work in recreation time. He was seated there now asleep. His superior touched him on the shoulder but Brother Paul made no response. The touch was followed by a word, but Brother Paul slept on.

Then the Prior's eye fell on the words traced just above the spot where the old head rested.

"Amen. Come, Lord Jesus."

He touched Brother Paul again, this time firmly, albeit that his hand shook. It was as he had guessed. The Lord had come quickly in response to the living cry of the Word scribed by Brother Paul with infinite pains at the completion of his labour of love.

# Chapter XIX

*Who Laughs Last——*

"CHRISTOPHER, Christopher! What hast thou done with the Christ?" The words rang in Christopher's ears as he rode along with Floss's head turned towards the forlorn pasture where he had left his flock grazing. What had possessed him to abandon them? His flock had need of the shepherd whose voice they had learnt to know. He had behaved like the hireling who turneth and fleeth. But God had taken pity on him and shown him his error. He must hasten back. There might be someone waiting—a saint, a sinner, a child at play. And the tardiest wight might be there. "Christopher! Christopher!"

But he must needs wait before taking the return journey. Floss, if not he, required a rest. There was the inn at the cross roads. He would pass the remainder of the night there.

The keeper of the inn was well used to late visitors. He had a bed available for the arrival. It was in the guest-chamber which was already occupied by another traveller, but he was a gentleman of quality and would not incommode the priest. Moreover, by this time he would be asleep.

Mine host was mistaken, however, about the second guest being asleep. He was, as a matter of fact, burning the midnight oil, though not with the same purpose as the monks.

The hours of darkness held haunting dreams for Master Catus, for it was he. His left arm was swathed in a bandage. Catus had been to Greathampton to consult a physician who was said to be skilled in the treatment of certain kinds of diseases. He had studied medicine in the east. The latter had examined the afflicted member. He had applied a hot iron to a sinister patch of white flesh, and Catus had felt no discomfort. The physician had questioned him. Haply his patient had been on pilgrimage in the Holy Land? Catus had disclaimed the notion that he had been on pilgrimage. He had no use for pilgrimages. Pious friends had suggested that he should apply a holy relic to his arm, as the leech had applied the hot iron, but he had long since lost his faith in saints and relics. His mind was as impervious as the white flesh.

Then haply Master Catus had been handling some of the documents that had recently been brought by scholars from the east? Infection could be carried that way. The physician feared that there was no doubt as to the nature of the malady; and no hope of a cure.

"You mean," Catus had said, bluntly, "that I am a leper, and that my flesh will rot away until I die?"

The other, having the professional manner of his own age, had replied. "I do mean that right enough, and may God have mercy on your soul."

Small wonder that the second traveller at the inn shrank from the lonely hours of the long, dark night.

Christopher creeping quietly up to his bed, was surprised to find the room lighted and his fellow traveller sitting up.

He recognised him with an exclamation of almost boyish pleasure. Master Catus was the very person whom he desired to meet. He had in his possession certain property belonging to Master Reginaldus which should have been returned to him a year ago. And by a curious chance he happened to have it with him now, in his wallet. Christopher did not intend to explain how this was the case. He produced the script delightedly from his wallet. He trusted Master Catus had not been incommoded by the temporary loss of the obit. He had left it with the Abbess of Gracerood to append her contribution, and it being just about the time that the good lady had been preoccupied about her charge, Petronilla de Lessels, between them they had failed to return it to Master Catus.

It was unfortunate that the latter was not in a mood to be amused, even by the vision of an Abbess swallowing St. Valarius at a gulp and adding to his panegyric. Human society, however, was very welcome, and the little parson's face was full of kindly concern as he scanned the other's and saw that there was something wrong.

"Have you a lazare in your parish?" Catus asked him, curtly. "I am seeking a lodging of that ilk."

He rolled up his sleeve, took off the bandage, and exhibited his arm.

Christopher gazed, with horrified eyes.

"You know what it is?" the other said.

"Yes, there was one that came to Bycross." Christopher's heart was full of pity for the man who had carried this secret about with him, and admiration for the grim courage which had kept it to himself. He was so very human although he did not belong to the party that called itself "humanist."

Catus was glad to have this very human being near him.

He had leant forward and raised the extended arm and was examining it gently, much as the physician had done, then, in the manner of those who practise a holy courtesy when they handle a sacred relic, he stooped and placed his lips to the spot that proclaimed the dread truth with the most uncompromising emphasis.

A swift, sudden light darted through his eyes.

"An' it be God's will," he said, "it will be made sound again."

"You believe in miracles," the sick man said, with a bitter twist of his mouth.

"I have known many to be worked," was the other's reply. He cast a swift glance at the M.S. lying near them.

"By St. Valarius?" Again there was the bitter twist of the mouth.

Christopher smiled serenely. "St. Valarius may see to it," he said. "We will pray hard this night. Haply Almighty God hath sent me here for that very purpose."

He was gently and not unskilfully replacing the bandage.

Master Catus said nothing. To a man in his sorry plight there is but poor consolation in the thought that he has won sixpence in a wager.

.        .        .        .        .

Christopher, having slept soundly after he had given himself permission to give over praying and do so, was wakened by a cry. He had been dreaming that someone was calling, "Christopher!" He woke with a start. Someone was calling. His companion was standing by his bedside. He had torn the bandage from his arm and was holding the latter out for inspection.

"There hath been a miracle," he said, huskily.

Christopher jumped up. He examined the arm carefully. It was absolutely as the other, save for a spot that might have been the prick of a pin, indicating the seat of the vanished horror.

"Thanks be to God," he said, simply. "He hath worked a very great miracle."

"And He hath worked it at your intercession," Catus said.

Christopher flushed. He avoided the other's eye. "St. Valarius," he stammered.

Catus fixed him hard with his eye.

"I invented St. Valarius," he said.

Christopher had been caught out. He ran his fingers frantically through his hair and confessed:

"I did guess that he had been invented for he was as many saints in one man, but I did not ween that it was by thee.

"'Tis like this," he went on, there was no hope for it—he must make a clean breast of it—"God, for His own mysterious reasons, hath seen fit to work many wonders for the people of my parish, and being but simple and unlettered they did take the notion into their foolish heads that the poor instrument that He used was—" Christopher was on the verge of tears—"had some hand in it. It did put my soul in great peril, this that the people were saying, and I could not make it that it were one of the saints that had obtained the favours, for that had been an offence to the saint being unsoothful. And then I thought me of the Abbot Valarius that might save me from the sin of vain-glory and eke take no hurt to himself, being no real person, but, such as any wight might invent."

Christopher had come to the end of his confession. He ventured to glance at the other's face. Had he given additional scandal to one who had taken sufficient scandal already?

Catus was thinking. "Sir Christopher," he said. "I did hear you preach a sermon about a year since of which methinks, I have a better understanding now than I had then."

The "obit" of the Abbot Valarius lay on the table.

"Let us see what the Abbess of Gracerood has to say," he said. "She may be less shrewd than thee in detecting a clumsy craftsman."

"I cannot tell thee," Christopher said, "for she hath written it in the Greek tongue."

Catus opened the roll. It was a thousand pities that the joke had lost its point, for it would seem that the Lady Abbess had fallen into the trap with a vengeance.

The writer, it appeared, however, had merely made use of the Greek characters. She was hardly airing her erudition, for what she had written was no bombastic original composition, but the following simple quotation:

> Hi diddle diddle the cat and the fiddle,
> The cow jumped over the moon.
> The little dog laughed to see the sport,
> And the dish ran after the spoon.

"She was passing anxious that I should return thee the script," Christopher said. "I know not what she hath written."

"I will translate it for you," Catus said.

So they sat and laughed and laughed, and the most authenticated "St. Valarius" could not have intervened more efficiently to relieve the pastor's head of its oppressive nimbus.

Then Master Catus took the script and added a last word. He wrote:

"Who laughs last laughs longest."

# Chapter XX

*Down with the Witch!*

THE RETURN to the wold might well have served to revive the memory of the vanished Petronilla in Humphrey Luffkyn's mind had it not been for the fact that it had never faded. Petronilla was as living and vivid a memory at the end of a year's flight as she had been when the distracted lover had scoured the wold in search of his missing lady-love.

Humphrey had never been the same since. He had matured suddenly. He wrote poetry which was read by the literary lights and approved. His friends wondered that he did not take to himself a sweetheart but it was laughingly said that Humphrey was too much in the clouds to wed anyone more substantial than a vision. His chief friend, Catus, indeed, himself wrote a poem telling of one that took to himself a færy wife, and that in the seeking of supreme union, each went forth by diverse ways into the land of dreams (Catus expressed it far more poetically than I can). And in that Land of Vision, behold, they walked, not divided but hand in hand. It was a fine poem and won Catus a prize at the University of Somewhere, a fantastic theme being permissible in these more enlightened days. Fantasy was fast becoming Catus's nearest approach to the Unseen.

Humphrey found Luffkynwold little to his taste. There was a brutality about its prosperity. The parson, to whom his heart went out in kinship, had fallen into bad odour with certain of his parishioners and they were saying detestable things that could only occur to base minds. It was in relation to the miserable creature whom they still called the witch, although she appeared to be quite harmless.

Humphrey had an experience of this ugly aspect of village life one afternoon soon after his arrival. He was walking near to the track which led to the hollow when he caught sight of a figure moving towards the cottage dressed in garments of the poorest description. As he was wondering if it might be the witch, an urchin darted out from the undergrowth and cast a handful of small stones at the retreating figure.

"Yah!" he shouted. "Yah! What hath thee done with the Dame de Lessels?"

Humphrey seized hold of him. "What art thou saying?" he demanded.

The boy began to whimper. "Tom Littlework do say that the witch did spirit away the lady that was being kept by the nuns."

"Pooh! Why should she do that?" Humphrey asked. "Let the poor soul be or I will make thee sorry."

"She thought the dame was rich," the boy answered. "She didn't know that she was a beggar any more than the dame did herself." He gave a nasty chuckle. Humphrey was within an ace of throttling him.

"But she was a beggar," he gurgled, justifying his position. "Be n't it true that she was but a beggar?"

It was a challenge that called for a refutation.

Humphrey paused, then delivered the strictly unlogical rejoinder not uncommonly resorted to in such circumstances. He administered a clout on the ear to the urchin in his grip. It would make him more careful in the future how he molested defenceless women.

Humphrey followed the retreating figure with his eyes. She was going very slowly. He wondered if she were wanting food. Poor soul. Luffkynwold was a foul and benighted spot for all that it had a saint for its pastor.

He waited until she had disappeared into the cottage. Then he went up quietly and placed a coin on the window-sill. On behalf, as it were, of one whose heart had been so tender towards beggars.

. . . . .

It was early on the following morning that Sir Robert Luffkyn sent for his son.

The blow had fallen. More heavily and completely than he had expected. The news had just arrived by special messenger.

He imparted it to Humphrey in characteristically few words.

"The King's ministers," he said, "have discovered the printing press at Bycross. They have likewise discovered that no press may be erected in England without a royal warrant."

"Then the Prior of Bycross will be getting into trouble," Humphrey said, in some alarm.

His father smiled grimly. "Not so; the Crown doth not seek to draw blood from a stone. It hath settled the crime on my head and I am to be bled white in the payment of the fine."

He named a sum the size of which left his son gasping.

It meant that Luffkynwold would be evacuated. Sir Robert had no further use for the soil which had borne his forebears. The wold might weep once more, or curse, or do what it would. The colony of workmen would be disbanded, the tannery abandoned, and Sir Robert would leave England and settle in Flanders, where he still had flourishing business interests.

"And the Hall?" Humphrey asked.

"I make you a present of it," his father said. He glanced at Humphrey with a gleam of cold humour in his eyes, "and you may marry the Lady Petronilla if you will."

The other sprang to his feet. "Then you will tell me where I may find her?" he cried. This was worth the loss of a dozen fortunes.

"That I know not any more than you," Sir Robert said. He might have expected his freakish son to take the loss of a fortune like this.

"But you told me that you had placed her in charge of some nuns."

"I told you no such thing," his father replied. "I did but wonder that the idea had not occurred to you. I am no liar."

"But I did tell the Abbess of Gracerood that it was so."

Sir Robert replied:

"I wished you to do so. Otherwise she would have believed worse."

Humphrey, in silence, took stock of his father. What a strange mixture he was. He felt a sudden pity for him. His dream had been shattered. And he had been a dreamer too. A lonely one. But the great outstanding matter was this.

Where was Petronilla?

Were her bones lying out on the cruel wold where she had gone in search of the beggar? Better that than that she should have followed in her mother's footsteps and become absorbed in the underworld into which the latter was supposed to have become immersed. Petronilla had strange blood in her veins.

It was at this crucial moment that they were interrupted by a noise under the window. There was a sound of many voices in the courtyard. What on earth could be the matter. The next moment their ears were assailed by a shout:

"Give us back Sir Christopher."

Sir Robert stared at his son. "What do they mean?" he asked.

The hasty appearance of John Appleyard explained matters.

Sir Christopher had gone on a journey and had asked Sir Amyas to say Mass in his church in his place. The foolish people had got the idea into their heads that Sir Christopher had been sent away and Sir Amyas put in his place. They had held the church door against the unoffending priest, who for his part, had retired in all haste, owing to a non-church-going section of the community who had armed themselves with brickbats and joined in the protest in order to show their good will to the parson.

There were rough customers in the village who were full willing to show their reverence for a holy man by breaking a head or two at a venture.

There had already been a free fight in the village between Sir Christopher's partisans and those who had lately been bringing grave charges against him. The latter accused him of keeping a wicked tryst with the witch out on the wold and the fury of the mob in general was directed against Astrotha the witch whose life was not at the present moment worth a day's purchase.

Once again the cry came up to them.

"Give us back our parson!"

Then, in a great volume of tone:

"We want Sir Christopher."

It was the first time that Luffkynwold had dictated to its lord.

Robert Luffkyn strode out. He flung open the great entrance door and stood before them. A hush fell on the crowd.

"Fools! Can a man give back that which he hath not taken away?"

There was a dead silence. Then a voice shouted from the back. "The witch hath spirited him away, the same as she did the Dame de Lessels."

Then there was a great roar from the crowd.

"Down with the witch!"

"Fools!"

This time it was not Sir Robert speaking, but his son. Humphrey stepped forward and glared round him.

"Do no harm to the witch, as you call her," he cried, "whilst Sir Christopher be not here to protect her. Do you not love him enough to take his word that she is no evil-doer?"

He flung an angry glance at the somewhat abashed faces. Then he turned to his father.

"I fear me that poor soul's life is in danger," he said. "I have a mind to go and give her a word of warning."

By this time Joan Luffkyn had appeared on the scene. Her mother was in discreet retirement receiving the reassurances of John Appleyard that it was not a peasant rising.

"Yes, Humphrey," she cried, "go quickly. 'Tis devilish the cruelty of the people to this one that they call a witch. I like not this place. And yet," Joan seemed uncertain, "it might be so holy."

Humphrey left his father to give her the tidings that full soon she would be pronounced free of the soil that exuded the things which pertain to the tainted cities. He made all haste towards the hollow, there was really no time to be lost. Joan was right. Luffkynwold was an unhallowed spot, or rather, dis-hallowed, for it had been holy in the old days. Perhaps in the days to come it would be holy again? In a sense it was holy. Wonders had been worked in Weepingwold (he preferred the old name). The parson, they said, invoked a saint whose intercession never failed. Humphrey recalled Catus and his unseemly jest. Poor Catus. Where was he now? And Joan was eating out her heart. If he were ill why did he not come and be cosseted by her? No one was so cunning at the making of simples for all disorders as his sister Joan. How happy she could have been in a Weepingwold that grew corn, and fed a generation of simple God-fearing folk to whom she could play the lady bountiful. Surely "Laughingwold" would be its right name then.

It was cold and cruel at present. And the wold, it might be, held the secret of Petronilla's disappearance. She had been at its mercy. He shuddered. Where was Petronilla? And he had lost all these months when he might have been seeking her.

As he neared the hollow he recognised a figure approaching him. It was the woman whom he had seen yesterday enter the cottage. Thank Heaven, he was just in time to tell her that it was madness for her to be abroad.

As she passed him, her head down, and the veil drawn closely about her face, he stopped her.

"Stay here," he told her hastily, "it is not safe for you to be abroad."

"I have one sick in my cottage," she replied. "I must fetch the priest."

"Sir Christopher is away," he said, "but I will send Sir Amyas."

She looked up quickly at his words. People said that the devil had given the witch back her youth and beauty. The face that looked up at his was youthful indeed! Almost that of a child. Of her beauty there could be no question.

"Petronilla!" he cried. "Petronilla!"

# Chapter XXI

## *Laughingwold*

S**HE STOOD THERE** before him, a startled look in her great grey eyes, the coarse black serge hood framing her face and concealing her hair, yet a more glorious Petronilla than the vision that he carried in his mind.

When at last she spoke she said:

"You are the first one that hath guessed it."

"And you have been Astrotha all the while?" he said. What was the meaning of it? He could but gaze at her and wonder if he were awake.

"I was Astrotha until last night," she replied. "Last night Astrotha returned—she that called herself Astrotha—and she lies yonder in the house, dying."

"Dying?" he repeated. "What hath happened to her?"

She answered:

"She was making her way hither when some cruel wretch did recognise her—one that had seen her aforetime—and cast a stone at her that hath done her a mortal hurt."

The speaker paused. "She managed to reach my hut," she went on, "and I did my best to dress her wound, but 'tis in her head, and I fear me that she is near death, and she hath yet to make her peace with God."

"She hath found an unexpected good Samaritan waiting her," Humphrey said.

"Yes, she thought to find the place empty"—it was like a dream to be hearing Petronilla speaking—"but I was here to give her a welcome. I knew she would come back one day."

He remained gazing at her, dazed and bewildered.

"Astrotha is not her real name?" he said.

"No."

"What is her real name?" He was asking questions vaguely—perhaps to make sure that he was not dreaming.

"Petronilla de Lessels. She is my mother."

She interrupted his look of astounded mystification. "Hark," she said, "I hear a horse's hoofs. I pray thee of thy charity run and see if it be Sir Christopher."

Her behest held good, as of yore, although Petronilla had learnt to say, "please." Humphrey ran back up the path. Sure enough it was Sir Christopher who was approaching. He had someone with him and the someone was—friend Catus!

The riders dismounted and Humphrey delivered his message.

"Astrotha hath returned," he said, "and Petronilla begs thee hasten to her aid for she hath been half murdered."

The priest asked no questions. He was off, down the path leading to the cottage.

Catus watched him. Then he turned to Humphrey. "Have no fear for the dying woman's soul," he said, "yon holy man can work miracles, and with souls as well as bodies."

Was this Catus? Humphrey surveyed his friend in wonder. He noted that he no longer carried his arm in a sling.

"Why dost thou think that?" he asked.

Catus lifted his cap. "He hath worked one on mine," he said.

"Ride as hard as you can to the hall," Humphrey said, a few minutes later, "and tell Joan that I have found Petronilla. And tell the people that Sir Christopher is back with them."

· · · · ·

Humphrey and Petronilla were standing outside the cottage.

Sir Christopher was within with Astrotha, and the latter was making her peace with God.

"And you have been here all the time?" Humphrey repeated.

She had been telling him of her discovery of the cell and the Cinderella outfit.

"Yea, it was a safe shelter. I had nowhere else to go when I did overhear Sir Christopher, out on the road, telling thee that the Mother Abbess would not receive me back."

He started. "You overheard that?"

"I feared that she would send me back to the world. I had a foolish notion about myself." She smiled. "But also I feared to return here, for people were saying that they had seen the witch about; but—" Petronilla smiled again—"I found that the witch that they had seen was no other than myself. The men that came along on horseback seeking me, did see my face and tell each other that it was the witch. And I marvelled why I should be so like her. And then I remembered that my mother had been an adventuress, and that her name was also Petronilla de Lessels, and I thought me of the name I had found with the garments in the chest; and it was all clear to me. So I went back and became, as it were, my own mother. I had a feeling"—she said this very slowly—"that some day she would return, and that I would fain be there to welcome her."

Humphrey was listening to the music of her voice. Could it be possible that he was again with Petronilla—the færie lady with whom Catus had linked him in his poem?

He watched her great, shadowed eyes. They were supplying for the words which she withheld. It was a very matured, and yet withal, a very simple Petronilla, this "penitent" who had play-acted her part for a whole year—a year and a day, to be exact.

As he watched a sudden thought struck him.

"Did you ever find the beggar?" he asked.

"Yea. But not for a long time—not till yesterday."

She was speaking very low, almost in a whisper.

"Yesterday?"

"Yea." She had decided to give him her confidence. She was feeling the kinship. "I had ever hugged a foolish fancy that Weepingwold was my inheritance." She smiled at him. "I thought it even up to yesterday. Then it happened that a child, casting stones at me, as they all did, called out, 'what hast thou done with the Dame de Lessels?' and hearing my name I listened. And I heard him speaking to one that had seized hold of him, and from what he said I learnt that the Dame de Lessels was but a beggar. He that was asked the question could not deny it, so I knew that soothly it was so."

She turned smiling eyes on the listener. "At first it was a dure shock to find that I had been a laughingstock to the world, and to ween that I had had nothing to renounce, being but a dreamer that had fled from a phantom. But when I came to understand that I was in very sooth a beggar, and not a great lady play-acting—when I found the penny on my window-sill—it seemed to me that One was standing there; and when I looked—it was He."

Petronilla's voice had dropped to an almost inaudible whisper. Humphrey waited patiently for the rest. But there was no more. She had honoured him thus far. They were wondrous close together. He tried to grasp the truth. Petronilla was here, a beggar, and he was there to say the word, if he only dared. He moved a little nearer. He was on holy ground. Dared he speak it?

A footstep sounded on the pathway behind them. She turned round quickly. It was as though the tip of a feather from the wing of an angel had brushed across his cheek.

Approaching them along the sloping path, the long skirt of her riding habit over her arm, was the small, alert figure of the Abbess of Gracerood. She was holding out her arms to the girl.

"Petronilla, my child!"

"Mother, Mother! God hath sent thee here."

The Abbess explained—in due course.

"Sir Christopher did bid me fetch thee."

"Sir Christopher?" the other echoed. "But he knows me only as Astrotha."

The Abbess smiled. "Sir Christopher hath played a trick on thee and on me. He hath sent me word that for a year and a day he hath kept thee here, serving thy novitiate; for I did yield him a promise that if thou hadst so proved thyself in some sufficiently dure novitiate I would receive thee into my family. This hath indeed been a dure novitiate, Petronilla. Come! Bring thy gift to God."

Petronilla looked up. "Holy Mother," she said. "I am but a beggar. I can ask of thee but a shelter, of thy charity for the love of God. I have nothing to give. Nothing to renounce, save beggary."

It was said, simply, eagerly, and very humbly.

The time had come for Humphrey to step forward.

"Not so," he declared. "Listen, good Mother Abbess, my father hath this day made me a gift of the ancient manor of Weepingwold, for which he has no more use. It is here for Dame Petronilla de Lessels to renounce as soothly as though it were her inheritance."

He stooped, took the hand of the kneeling girl, and raising her placed it between the outstretched hands of the Abbess.

Catus's færie poem had suddenly come true. The parting of the ways would lead them to a country where they would walk hand-in-hand. He was looking out upon it now, through a window which was Petronilla's soul.

Their eyes met for a moment. There were indeed great possessions for Petronilla to renounce.

Then, next moment, the Abbess had opened her arms and Petronilla was folded within them.

"My child," she cried. "My child! Oh, my child!"

.     .     .     .     .

Inside the cottage Sir Christopher was helping the witch to make her peace with God. He had heard her confession, that same confession which he had thought to listen to that other time when Petronilla had come to him. He had not recognised her at first. Then, when he had done so he had held his peace. Even his fingering might, perchance, have soiled the dazzling whiteness of the garment which she had set herself to weave for the Christ-Child.

The dying woman told him her story. She had returned in order to possess herself of some papers which she discovered she had left in the chest. They told much of her past life and of her identity. In the wood, near her destination, she had received the fatal blow from an unseen hand. She had struggled to the cottage that she might lie down and die, and there she had been met by a ministering angel. An angel who was the likeness of herself as she might have been. The hermit's cell had been full of holy magic. The child whom she had abandoned in the cradle was there awaiting her, representing all that she herself might have been had she followed the greater adventure. In a way, she had represented her before God here, in this place, for a year and a day. Mariquita, who was also Petronilla de Lessels, had become entoiled in the hermit's spell. The hermit had conquered. She had cried out to make her peace with God.

When she had fallen into a gentle sleep Christopher left her side and came out. He would send Petronilla back to her.

The first person that his eyes fell on was the Mother Abbess. Petronilla and Humphrey were standing by her side and she held a hand of each, dividing them, as it were, and eke uniting them. The King's Mother leading them to her Son—so little Brother Kit pictured it.

He stood a moment watching. Mother Abbess would smile when she saw the wandering shepherd returned to the fold, like the sheep of little Bo-peep! But he would smile back at her, caught in the snare of her own pledged word.

And all the wold around seemed to be filled with holy mirth. It was laughing at Master Catus, riding at top speed to his lady love— the last laugh which is the longest. It was laughing with Humphrey and Petronilla and the spirit of the holy hermit, for it has been said by somebody that the sacring bell which rings before the sacrifice is every whit as merrie as the marriage bell.

And so Humphrey and Petronilla found it in the days to come.

.     .     .     .     .

It was a sobered and somewhat shamefaced assembly that witnessed the burial of the ex-witch some few days later. The Abbess of Gracerood herself had visited the penitent, and, it was said, had sent one of her own daughters to tend her at the end. Luffkynwold was properly ashamed of itself.

They laid her close to the little chancel window where she had once "peeped out" into a large place, and the memory of Astrotha was as of one who had "made good," in the sight of men, and I durst say also, in the sight of angels, for such is the teaching and preaching of Holy Church.

# Epilogue

OMEWHERE in the second decade of the sixteenth century a painstaking topographer, in making a survey of the country round Greathampton, thus describes the village at one time known as Weepingwold.

"To the right lieth the village which is called by the vulgar 'Laughingwold,' which is a corruption of Luffkynwold, the name given to Weepingwold by a former Lord of the Manor, Sir Robert Luffkyn who established a tannery here for a space. The tannery hath long since disappeared, for the present Lord of the Manor, the world-famed Master Reginaldus Catus, whose good lady is a daughter of the said Sir Robert Luffkyn, and a sister of the holy and learned Prior Humphrey of Bycross Priory, prefereth to grow corn, which he doth in so great quantities that all the world cometh to see his golden lands.

"Seeing that Master Catus is a man of merry wit as well as of mighty learning—scarce less so than Mr. Justice More himself—it hath been aptly said that the ancient prophecy which runneth:

> When Weepingwold hath a laughing lord
> Treasure of gold shall he watch and ward—

hath found its fulfilment.

"The church possesseth the finest spire in the county, which same was erected by the people of the village, many of whom were masons and artificers who remained behind when the others left, deeming it a goodlier thing to grow corn for the altar breads than to wax rich in a town. For the piety and good-living of the people of this village is the marvel of all that come this way. The parson, Sir Christopher Plimsett, hath held the benefice a full thirty years.

"The church containeth many objects of value, the gifts of parishioners, whose names are recorded on the bede-roll. The silken shirt worn by the image of the Holy Child is said to be the gift of the Abbess of Gracerood, but which Abbess I was not told. But seeing that it is of spotless white silk, new and untarnished, the donor would appear to be the newly-appointed Abbess, Dame Petronilla de Lessels."

# THE END

# ALSO BY ENID DINNIS

*View sample chapters from each title at www.staidanpress.com or on Amazon.com.*

## THE ANCHORHOLD
*by Enid Dinnis*

Editha de Beauville had all that the world could offer: wealth, wit, and beauty. Yet a chaplain's sermon drove her to give up all this, and enter the religious life. But could a proud, strong-willed noblewoman accept and embrace the poverty and self-abnegation of the religious life, particularly that of full seclusion in an anchorhold? A difficult path lay before Editha. Read on to learn how she fared, and how her life affected those around her, including Sir Aleric, her erstwhile suitor, now a crusader knight; Fr. Nicholas, a young priest who was quite bright, and thought so too; and Fiddlemee, the witty yet wise court jester whose past held a surprising secret.

$14.00 — 194 pages. Available at amazon.com.

# OTHER TITLES AVAILABLE FROM ST. AIDAN PRESS

## THE NET
*by Agnes Blundell*

"Roger felt a freezing dew break out upon his forehead. The net was over him it seemed; in vain he told himself that he could establish his identity. His head was worth forty pounds to the vile creatures at the stair foot, and once in their clutches who knew if he could ever communicate with his friends? . . . Gaolers and pursuivants alike fattened on the traffic in human life and divided the spoils. Judges were as careless as callous."

$16.00 — 264 pages. Available at amazon.com

## SCOUTING FOR SECRET SERVICE
*by Fr. Bernard F. J. Dooley*

Frank and George are going to spend their summer vacation in the Adirondacks, thanks to Frank's uncle Ed. But once they get there, they realize something fishy is going on. Can they trust Pete, their Indian guide, or is he mixed up in it too? And is Frank's mysterious uncle really behind it all?

$14.00 — 188 pages. Available at amazon.com.

## THE HAPPINESS OF FATHER HAPPÉ
*by Cecily Hallack*

Shingle Bay did not know what to make of Fr. Savinius Happé. He was a cheerful, rotund Franciscan, a famous author of books on everything from Etruscan civilization to Alpine meadows to beetles, and someone who had never quite mastered the English language. His jovial demeanor concealed a wisdom that alternately bewildered, astonished, but ultimately won over the people of Shingle Bay.

$10.00 — 112 pages. Available at amazon.com.

## CON OF MISTY MOUNTAIN
*by Mary T. Waggaman*

"It had been a long night for Con. Just what had happened to him he was at first too dazed to know. Dennis had flung him into the smoking-room with no very gentle hand, turned the key and left him to himself. And, sinking down dully upon a rug that felt very soft and warm after the hard flight over the mountain, Con was glad to rest his bruised, aching limbs, his dizzy head, without any thought of what was to come upon him next."

$14.00 — 190 pages. Available at amazon.com.